Short Bike Rides™
in and around
Washington, D.C.

Help Us Keep This Guide Up to Date

Every effort has been made by the author and editors to make this guide as accurate and useful as possible. However, many things can change after a guide is published—establishments close, biking trails are rerouted, etc.

We would love to hear from you concerning your experiences with this guide and how you feel it could be made better and be kept up to date. While we may not be able to respond to all comments and suggestions, we'll take them to heart, and we'll also make certain to share them with the author. Please send your comments and suggestions to the following address:

The Globe Pequot Press
Reader Response/Editorial Department
P.O. Box 833
Old Saybrook, CT 06475

Or you may e-mail us at:

editorial@globe-pequot.com

Thanks for your input, and happy travels!

Short Bike Rides™ Series

Short Bike Rides™ in and around Washington, D.C.

Fourth Edition

by Michael Leccese

Revisions by Edward M. Reardon

Old Saybrook, Connecticut

Photo Credits
Pp. x, 12: Bill Clark, courtesy of National Park Service; pp. 4–5: Fred Fizell, courtesy of D.C. Development Land Agency/National Park Service; pp. 16, 41, 46, 100, 122, 140, 153, 176: courtesy of Edward M. Reardon; p. 90: Paul Thomas; pp. 28, 124: courtesy of Historic American Buildings Survey; p. 30: Jack Rottier, courtesy of National Park Service; pp. 48, 64: courtesy of National Park Service; pp. 70–71: courtesy of Library of Congress; pp. 76–77: © Charles Votaw; p. 82: courtesy Montgomery County Historical Society; p. 88: courtesy of United States National Arboretum; p. 104: Paul Souders, *The Montgomery Journal;* pp. 136–37: M. Woodbridge Williams, courtesy of National Park Service; p. 156: Cecil W. Stoughton, courtesy of National Park Service; pp. 188–89: courtesy RTKL.

Cover design: Saralyn D'Amato-Twomey
Cover photo: Chris Dubé
Maps design: MAry Ballachino

Short Bike Rides is a trademark of The Globe Pequot Press.

Library of Congress Cataloging-in-Publication Data
Leccese, Michael.
    Short Bike Rides in and around Washington D.C. / by Michael
Leccese, Edward M. Reardron. — 4th ed.
            p. cm.
    Includes bibliographical references and index.
    ISBN 0–7627–0335–0
    1. Bicycle touring—Washington Metropolitan Area—Guidebooks.
    2. Washington Metropolitan Area—Guidebooks. I. Reardon, Edward M.
    II. Title.
    GV1045.5.W18L43   1998
    917.5304'41—DC21   98-27572
                                                              CIP

Manufactured in the United States of America
Fourth Edition/First Printing

Contents

Overview of Rides by Category

		Tourists	Families w/ Children
1	Monuments on the Waterfront	●	●
2	Monuments on the Mall	●	short version
3	Rock Creek Park: D.C.	●	●
4	Rock Creek Park: D.C. to Maryland & Back	●	weekends
5	Capital Crescent Loop	●	weekends
6	W&OD Trail through Virginia Countryside		
7	Mount Vernon Trail: D.C. to Old Town		●
8	Old Town to Mount Vernon	●	●
9	Rosemont Ramble	●	
10	Reservoir—Great Falls Run	●	
11	Upper Reaches of Rock Creek Park		
12	Sligo–Rock Creek Weekend Loop	●	weekends
13	National Arboretum Loop-de-Loop	●	●
14	C&O Canal: Georgetown to Great Falls	●	●
15	Tour of South Arlington	●	●
16	Tour of North Arlington	●	
17	Neighborhoods of Northwest D.C.	with caution	
18	Dupont–Georgetown–Cleveland Park Loop	●	
19	Prince William Forest Park	●	
20	Prince George's Urban Farmland	●	●
21	Two Creeks of Maryland		●
22	Around Avenel: A Piece of Potomac		
23	To Edward's Ferry	●	canal route
24	Sugarland Loop		
25	Escape to Maryland Countryside		
26	The Three-State Special	●	
27	Hardly Hilly Hunt Country Tour	●	
28	Winery and Woods	●	
29	Blue Ridge Splendor	●	
30	To the Races	●	
31	Historic Waterford	●	

Natural Beauty	Mostly Bike Paths	Countryside	Workout	
				1
				2
●	●			3
●	●			4
●	●			5
●	●	●	●	6
●	●	●		7
●	●			8
				9
●				10
●			●	11
●	●			12
●				13
●	●	●		14
	●			15
●				16
				17
				18
●		●		19
●		●		20
●	●	●		21
●		●		22
●	●	●		23
●		●		24
●		●	●	25
●		●	●	26
●		●	●	27
●		●	●	28
●		●	●	29
●		●	●	30
●		●	●	31

Introduction

Washington, D.C., and environs are an urban cyclist's dream. The metropolitan area of 3 million people finds room for 48,080 acres of parkland and more than 670 miles of paved, off-road multiuse trails. The city and its suburbs have also designated 480 miles of signed on-road bike routes. And if weather turns foul, cyclists can (with a proper pass) jump on Metrorail, the region's 70-mile subway system, which sells bicycle passes good during non–rush hours on weekdays and all day on weekends and most holidays.

Starting from the city's social and historic center, Georgetown, you could ride to Mount Vernon (16 miles); the foothills of the Blue Ridge Mountains (60 miles); Cumberland, Maryland (180 miles); or the Oz-like Mormon Temple (10 miles)—while encountering hardly a single automobile. Staying within city boundaries, you could visit the Lincoln Memorial, White House, Smithsonian museums, and U.S. Capitol, all within one hour of easy pedaling.

Not surprising for a city of political activists, Washington boasts the nation's largest regional bicycle club, the Potomac Pedalers Touring Club (PPTC), and its own two-wheeled transportation lobby, the Washington Area Bicyclists Association (WABA). In 1988 *Bicycling* magazine named D.C. one of the top ten U.S. cities for cyclists. In 1998 the League of American Bicyclists (LAB) moved their national headquarters to Washington, D.C., where they have better access to policy-makers affecting cyclists in America. First formed in 1880 as the League of American Wheelmen, LAB promotes bicycling for recreation and transportation.

In *Captive Capital* (Indiana University Press, 1974) Sam Smith describes Washington as ". . . one of the most attractive, civil, interesting and pleasant [cities] in the country." Geography is part of what makes it so. Washington is located at the confluence of two rivers, where the coastal plain collides with the Piedmont foothills. Near the city line, the Potomac rushes over Class VI ("risk-of-life") rapids to meet estuary waters lapping up from the Chesapeake Bay. The old Federal City sits low on former swampland; the newer outskirts rise as high as 400 feet on bluffs overlooking the Potomac.

If Washington seems an anomaly among U.S. cities, perhaps it is because it is a planned city, founded by congressional fiat in 1790 and laid out by the brilliant, stormy French engineer, Pierre Charles L'Enfant. L'Enfant based his baroque street plan on elements of eighteenth-century London, Paris, and Rome. Much of his vision survives: the broad avenues cutting diagonally across a grid of streets, the stunning vistas of monuments, and the abundant groves of trees.

L'Enfant conceived a diamond-shaped city 10 miles square, divided into four quadrants: Northwest, Southwest, Northeast, and Southeast. This can cause confusion. There is both a 1000 Pennsylvania Avenue N.W. and a 1000 Pennsylvania Avenue S.E.; there are two A Streets with near-identical addresses, four First Streets, and so on. In 1846 Arlington County and Alexandria reverted to the Commonwealth of Virginia, leaving the Potomac River as a natural boundary for the Northwest and Southwest quadrants.

Predating the founding of Washington were the eighteenth-century ports of Georgetown and Alexandria. Today these national historic districts are the focus of tourism. Both feature cobblestone alleys, colonial houses, cozy narrow streets, and excellent access by bicycle. You can still find one of the city's original boundary markers on Alexandria's edge.

Since 1966 the metropolitan area has been shaped by a new boundary that has effectively extended the city limits: the Beltway, a 66-mile superhighway looping around Washington. The Beltway can be a cyclist's bane, since it blocks many pedaling routes out of the city. This book will attempt to be your passkey through its concrete fortifications.

Freeways aside, D.C. has some of the nation's strictest zoning and planning laws. As a result of a 1910 law, no building may rise higher than twelve stories, or about 130 feet. Development near parks and public buildings is subject to review by the Fine Arts Commission. Here you find an asset rarely visible in Manhattan or even Pittsburgh: the horizon.

Culture in all its forms enlivens life in the nation's capital. Easily accessible by bicycle are all the monuments, more than 150 embassies, the Kennedy Center, 70 museums, colonial historic districts, and restaurants ranging from Afghani to Vietnamese. As the city population is nearly 70 percent African-American, it is also home to an African-American university, several museums of African-American history and art, and landmarks such as Cedar Hill, the former residence of abolitionist Frederick Douglass, now owned and interpreted by the National Park Service. Moreover, there are Hispanic neighborhoods in Mount Pleasant and Adams-Morgan, a Vietnamese section in Arlington, and a vestigial Italian area downtown.

During the time I've lived in Washington, I've probably clocked more mileage on a dozen bicycles (from L'Enfant, an electric-blue ten-speed rescued from the trash, to Velo, an eighteen-speed touring model I once rode from Austria to England) than in my car. In general, life has improved for local cyclists during that time. For example, the National Park Service spent $1.5 million on an elevated path near Theodore Roosevelt Island, thus connecting two routes and creating one of the nation's longest contiguous bikeways. The 64-mile path connects Mount Vernon with the Blue Ridge foothills to the west.

Today, cycling in the Washington area seems poised for a breakthrough. Fed up with traffic and pollution, regional governments are weighing a $60 million plan to connect regional trails and lanes into a 1,000-mile system complete with standardized signs—a sort of interstate system for bicyclists.

This ambitious plan recognizes that a bicycle is an environmental tool. I hope readers will use this book not only for pleasure rides but also to plot rides to work, to run errands, and to visit friends and family. In some small way, you'll directly prevent pollution and ease the demand for more highways and parking lots. And yes, you'll save lots of money, too—fewer repair bills, insurance premiums, or payments for a second car.

That said, this region could be far more hospitable to bikers. There have been setbacks: D.C. eliminated the position of bicycle coordinator from their city government. And the suburbs continue to sprawl with relatively little regard for either bicyclists or pedestrians.

I urge readers of this guide to become advocates of bicycle trans-

portation. Join the Washington Area Bicyclists Association and the League of American Bicyclists. Lobby your workplace to install a shower and safe bicycle parking. (Many offices already have a shower, installed long ago by some jogging executive. Ask your office manager to remove the old files so that you can reclaim the space.)

Be sure that your local, county, and state representatives know you support bicycling. Find out what trails are being planned and state your support for them. Here are two for starters: the Metropolitan Branch from Union Station to Silver Spring and the continuation of Capital Crescent from Silver Spring to Bethesda (the paved segment from Bethesda to Georgetown was completed in 1995; hardpacked gravel trails still remain between Bethesda and Silver Spring). Build those two, and Washington will have a Bicycle Beltway.

A word on safety

The biker looking to conquer the capital should take some precautions, such as the following:

1. Wear a helmet. Traffic here is insistent, swift, and sometimes abusive to cyclists. If that's not reason enough, try this: Once someone tossed a bottle at my head when I was riding through the Adams-Morgan neighborhood. It struck my helmet and shattered. Without the hard hat, I'd still be picking shards of glass from my scalp.

2. Buy the strongest U-shaped lock you can find. Bicycles are more likely to be stolen than cars here. Be sure to secure both wheels and the frame to a fixture such as a bolt-down bike rack or a double parking meter. Better yet, bring the bike indoors or lock it in a parking garage.

3. Carry maps. The bikeways have been improved, but the rivers, train tracks, and freeways form many obstacles and dead ends. The city's quadrant system can easily confuse newcomers. All too often, meandering cyclists find themselves on four-lane roads or two-laners with blind curves and no shoulders. It isn't worth the risk, and there's usually a better way through. (The maps included in this book should help greatly. If you do veer off the routes, a good local map will help you get righted.)

Note: A new feature on the maps—R—indicates restroom locations.

4. Realize that off-road multi-use trails aren't for bikes alone. Despite common terminology, they are *not* exclusively "bike paths." Share them courteously with families out for a stroll, hikers, and in-line skaters, as well as other cyclists.

5. Take a buddy. Washington's violent crime problems have been well publicized, and while I've never felt afraid, I would advise cyclists to ride in pairs and carry spare parts and tubes.

About the directions

All rides include step-by-step directions and maps. Starting points can be reached by auto or Metrorail and are often near bike-rental facilities. See the section about obtaining a Metrorail Bike-on-Rail permit.

Some of the rides (23 and 24, for example) may be combined into longer routes. While some rides are planned as loops, others are one-way rides that require doubling back the way you came. In the latter cases, I've tried to include optional side-trips to historic or scenic sites that will vary the scenery on the return trip.

Rides 25 through 31 are longer and more challenging trips. Novice or out-of-shape cyclists should try the shorter rides first.

Local cycling clubs and regional park authorities can help plan rides. Most publish maps. Some even organize weekend rides. I've included a list of cycling sources in the Appendix.

Off-road cycling

If you bought a bike in recent years, chances are it was an all-terrain or mountain bike. For routes suitable for all-terrain bikes, see Rides 11, 14, 19, and 23. When riding an ATB, take care not to trespass on hiking trails or disturb wildlife areas. As these types of conflicts increase, the National Park Service and other park authorities are banning knobby-tire bikes in many areas.

A word on climate

Washington's summers can only be described as torrid. The typical August mercury hovers around 95 degrees, with comparable humidity. Moreover, the summer air quality can be atrocious. During many summer days the pollution (most of it generated by the area's millions of cars) makes exercise unhealthful.

The region atones for the intolerable summer season with lingering warm autumns and springs and mild winters. To wit, I tested most of the rides included in this book during a particularly sunny January with temperatures of about 50 degrees.

You can beat the summer heat by rising early to complete short rides before 9:00 A.M. Owning a bike pass for Metrorail also comes in handy. When the sun drops and the wind rises at about 6:00 P.M., I like to take off for Mount Vernon, timing the trip so that I arrive at Alexandria's King Street station at about sunset. The air-conditioned ride home is particularly refreshing.

Monuments on
the Waterfront

Distance:	13-mile loop
Approximate pedaling time:	90 minutes
Terrain:	Flat except for Arlington Cemetery
Surface:	Good paths, roads, and sidewalks
Things to see:	FDR Memorial, Tidal Basin, Hains Point, Jefferson Memorial, Arlington Cemetery, Lincoln Memorial, Korean War Veterans Memorial, Vietnam Veterans Memorial
Facilities:	Rest rooms, snack bars, and souvenir stands at the monuments and cemetery
Recommended for:	Tourists, Families with children

This ride along the D.C. and Virginia banks of the Potomac River could take weeks if you savored all the riches en route. This is Washington at its most Athenian.

Start at the Harry T. Thompson Boat Center, where you can rent boats and bikes (March to November). If you are arriving by car and parking here, be aware of the three-hour limit in this metered lot. Head southeast on a bikeway that runs past the Watergate Apartments and between the Kennedy Center and the Potomac River. Built in 1970 on the site of the Heurich Brewery, the 630-foot-long performing arts center contains the American Film Institute movie theater, an opera house, a stage for major plays, a concert hall, a cabaret, and restaurants.

After riding past volleyball courts and through two narrow bridge underpasses (dismounting recommended), you will arrive in 1.3 miles within view of the Lincoln Memorial, at the John Ericsson Monument

9

Dupont Circle

NORTH

Park &
START

Thompson
Boat Center
R

White House

ROOSEVELT
ISLAND

Kennedy Ctr.

Pennsylvania Ave.

U.S. Capitol

Lincoln R
Memorial

Washington
Monument

National Mall
& Smithsonian
Museums

Memorial Bridge

Arlington Cemetery

Ericsson Monument

Arlington House
(Lee Mansion) R

Roosevelt Memorial R

Memorial Dr.

POTOMAC

TIDAL
BASIN

Jefferson Memorial R

Sherman Dr.

Buckeye Dr.

Meigs Ave.

Mt. Vernon Trail

1909
Bridge

WASHINGTON CHANNEL

Fort Myer Gate
(turnaround)

VIRGINIA

HAINS
PT. R

RIVER

Ohio Dr.

ANACOSTIA RIVER

Pentagon

14th
Street
Bridge

Reagan National Airport

HOW
to get
there

From north, Rock Creek Parkway south to
Thompson's parking lot; turn right. From Mall, Virginia
Avenue west across Rock Creek Parkway to Thompson's
parking lot. From Virginia, Theodore Roosevelt Bridge or
Memorial Bridge to Rock Creek Parkway to Thompson's parking
lot. By Metro, Blue or Orange Line to Foggy Bottom/GWU, about a
1-mile walk or ride. From Metro station, walk south on Twenty-third
Street (away from Washington Circle). Turn right on H Street, left on
New Hampshire Avenue, and right on Virginia Avenue. Cross Rock
Creek Parkway at crosswalk to reach parking lot of Thompson Boat
Center. Follow one-lane road over short bridge to waterfront.

DIREC-TIONS
for the ride

- From Thompson Boat Center, right on trail heading toward Watergate Apartments and Kennedy Center, Potomac River on right.
- Cross parkway intersection to reach path. Continue between outdoor volleyball courts.
- Ride (or dismount and walk) through two short bridge underpasses. Bear right with bike path onto Ohio Drive at Ericsson Monument.
- Proceed southeast for 0.8 mile on Ohio Drive past Roosevelt Memorial on left. Cross 1909 bridge. Turn right and follow signs to East Potomac Park (Hains Point).
- Cross under four bridges. Left at stop sign onto Buckeye Drive to begin loop of East Potomac Park.
- Right at stop sign onto Ohio Drive.
- At end of one-way loop, keep straight on Ohio Drive. Pass under four bridges. Do not cross 1909 bridge. Bear right toward Jefferson Memorial.
- Across from parking-lot entrance to Memorial, access Fourteenth Street Bridge bike path via curb cut on right.
- Cross bridge and bear right on bike path. Turn left at T.
- Proceed upriver on Mount Vernon Trail past Navy and Marine Memorial and Lady Bird Johnson Park.
- To reach Arlington Cemetery bear left at fork in trail and cross George Washington Parkway three times at crosswalks marked with stripes.
- At Memorial Drive, stay on sidewalk. Detour to visitor's center on left.
- At end of Memorial Drive turn right on Schley Avenue. Continue uphill via Sherman and Meigs Avenues to Fort Myer gates. Turn around and return to Memorial Drive.
- Using Memorial Bridge sidewalk, cross to D.C. to Lincoln Memorial.
- Take unmarked road back to Ericsson Monument.
- Retrace path back to Thompson's.

at Independence Avenue and Ohio Drive S.W. Carved from granite and dedicated in 1926, the Ericsson statue pays tribute to the designer of the U.S.S. *Monitor,* the ironclad warship that fought the Confederate ironclad *Merrimac* during the Civil War.

View the Lincoln Memorial in profile and proceed downriver on Ohio Drive, with the polo fields of West Potomac Park on your left and the Tidal Basin beyond. (Time your ride for a summer Sunday afternoon if you want to watch part of a polo match.)

Washington's newest monument, the Franklin Delano Roosevelt Memorial, is along this stretch of Ohio Drive. Opened in 1997, it joins the memorials to Washington, Jefferson, and Lincoln as major tributes to four great American leaders. Rather than a grand marble structure, the Roosevelt Memorial consists mainly of a series of contemplative outdoor gardens.

Approximately 0.8 mile ahead lies a brief but graceful bridge stamped 1909 and ornamented with gargoyle fountains. Cross it and turn right at the circular flower bed to stay on Ohio Drive. Pass under four bridges for automobiles, Amtrak, and Metrorail, and then begin a 3-mile, one-way loop around East Potomac Park, a popular picnic area that features an Olympic-size pool, a golf course, and many flowering trees.

At the park's apogee is Hains Point, fronting the confluence of the Potomac and Anacostia Rivers and Washington Channel, a waterway full of pleasure boats. Across the channel lies old Fort McNair and its impressive brick buildings. The tall, domed edifice is the Army War College, founded by Theodore Roosevelt after the Spanish-American War. Reagan National Airport is directly over the Potomac.

Hains Point beckons when you see huge fingers and a large bearded head rising from the ground. The startling figure is Seward Johnson's 1980 statue "The Awakening," which portrays a Brobdingnagian figure rising from the soil. Have your photo taken perched on one of the large aluminum digits, then proceed upstream, parallel to the Potomac River.

Return via the loop to the 1909 bridge. Instead of crossing, turn right toward the Jefferson Memorial. Built in 1943, this domed pavilion ringed by fifty-four columns houses a 19-foot-tall bronze statue of

Thomas Jefferson and inscriptions of his words. The memorial fronts the Tidal Basin and its famous crescent of cherry trees, whose early-April blooms are cause for citywide celebration.

Returning to the parking-lot entrance, look for a curb cut leading to a bike path over the Fourteenth Street (George Mason Memorial) Bridge. The bikeway over the span is an engineering marvel—wide, smooth, and well-protected from the main roadway. You'll have views of the Pentagon, sailboats, and bridges carrying Metrorail and freight trains over the river. At the base of the bridge on the Virginia side, bear right onto the Mount Vernon Trail, which parallels the George Washington Memorial Parkway. Take an immediate left to begin your return upriver.

With the Potomac on your right and Boundary Channel on your left, pedal a quarter of a mile and over a little bridge to the graceful Navy and Marine Memorial, dedicated to Americans lost at sea. Ride a few hundred feet more to the southern edge of Lady Bird Johnson Park. Designated in 1968 to honor the arboreal-minded First Lady, the island park is planted with 2,700 dogwoods and 1 million daffodils (carefully counted, according to the National Park Service). Just over the parkway (a dicey crossing for cyclists) stands Columbia Island Marina and the fifteen-acre Lyndon Baines Johnson Memorial Grove, planted with hundreds of white pine trees surrounding a memorial stone shaped from pink Texas granite. Continue on the trail toward Arlington Memorial Bridge, dedicated in 1932 to symbolize the reunion of North and South. Bear left on the trail to avoid passing under the bridge, and ford two striped crosswalks across the George Washington Memorial Parkway. Cross a traffic circle to reach Memorial Drive, gateway to Arlington National Cemetery.

Ride on the sidewalk to avoid the macadam road surface. Pause to ponder "The Hiker," a 1965 statue dedicated to veterans of the Spanish-American War of 1898. Across the road is the Seabees Memorial; note their proud "Can Do" motto. The cemetery's visitor's center is on the left, halfway down Memorial Drive. Lock your bike to one of the iron gates (no bike racks) if you want to go inside for information.

At the massive stone gate marking the end of Memorial Drive, turn right on Schley Avenue to make a short tour of the grounds. The route is well marked, as are roads off-limits to bikes. Continue up Schley to Meigs Avenue, which leads to the Lee Mansion (Arlington House) high on a precipice with a view of the river and the monuments of Washington. This is a good place to park and explore the cemetery on foot. On the way back, visit a marker honoring city planner Pierre L'Enfant. This spot offers a magnificent view of downtown Washington. Then retrace your ride back to the Memorial Bridge.

Gingerly cross the traffic circle again to reach the bridge's sidewalk, which you can ride back to Washington. Pass by the two enormous, golden equestrian statues symbolizing Valor and Sacrifice, and bear right at the end of the sidewalk. Again, carefully make your way across the traffic circle (preferably on foot) to the Lincoln Memorial grounds.

Built in 1922 to honor the author of the Emancipation Proclamation, the Memorial has since been a magnet for civil rights activism. Here, in 1939, black singer Marian Anderson performed her famous concert, defiant of segregation, and in 1963 Martin Luther King uttered his "I Have a Dream" speech to a throng of 200,000. Architect Henry Bacon designed the building in the style of a Greek temple with Roman detailing. Sculptor Daniel Chester French created the 900-ton figure of Lincoln from twenty-eight blocks of white Georgia marble. Beneath the Memorial lies a catacomb created by the construction. It's actually filled with stalactites and stalagmites formed by water dripping from the marble steps.

Flanking the Lincoln Memorial, and directly across from the Vietnam Veterans Memorial, is the site of the Korean War Veterans Memorial, a monumental landscape that features life-size-plus statues of soldiers marching across a reflecting pool. The memorial was dedicated in 1995.

Now you can either return to Thompson's or pick up the second leg of this monumental tour in Ride 2.

Monuments on the Mall

Distance:	9.7-mile loop
Approximate pedaling time:	90 minutes
Terrain:	Flat except for Capitol Hill
Surface:	Roads and paved paths
Things to see:	Washington Monument, Smithsonian museums, U.S. Capitol, Library of Congress, Union Station, the White House, Vietnam Veterans Memorial
Facilities:	Rest rooms, gift shops, restaurants, and bike racks at most museums and Union Station.
Recommended for:	Shorter version suitable for all. Longer version requires riding in traffic; lighter on weekends.

This tour combines the great houses of government with the great houses of knowledge. I doubt that even Manhattan could boast of such a concentration of cultural institutions and world-class landmarks.

Begin at the Harry T. Thompson Boat Center (bike rentals available March to November). If you are arriving by car and parking here, be aware of the three-hour limit in this metered lot. Proceed to the Lincoln Memorial as described in Ride 1. Ride to the east steps of the Lincoln Memorial for a stunning view of an axis that includes the Washington Monument and, nearly 2 miles away, the U.S. Capitol.

Head down a slight slope past a souvenir stand on your right to pick up a path parallel to the 0.5-mile-long Reflecting Pool. Continue past the fountains (filled with mallard ducklings in spring) and jog to the left on the sidewalk to reach the pedestrian crossing at busy Seventeenth Street.

Park &
START

★ Thompson ℝ
Boat Center

17th St. N.W.

E. Executive Ave.

13th St. N.W.

Penn. Ave. N.W.

The White
House

Constitution Ave.

Louisiana Ave.

● Union Station ℝ

Columbus Circle

Capitol Hill
Neighborhood

First St.

11th St. N.W.

Constitution Ave.
Lincoln Memorial
Reflecting Pool ℝ

Washington
● Monument

Madison Dr.

U.S.
Capitol

E. Capitol St.

Lincoln Park

Jefferson Dr.

3rd St.

Independence Ave.

TIDAL
BASIN

North Carolina
Ave.

Eastern | Market

NORTH

POTOMAC

RIVER

ANACOSTIA RIVER

HOW
to get
there

From north, Rock Creek Parkway south to
Thompson's parking lot; turn right. From Mall, Virginia
Avenue west across Rock Creek Parkway to Thompson's
parking lot. From Virginia, Theodore Roosevelt Bridge or
Memorial Bridge to Rock Creek Parkway to Thompson's parking
lot. By Metro, Blue or Orange Line to Foggy Bottom/GWU, about a
1-mile walk or ride. From Metro station, walk south on Twenty-third
Street (away from Washington Circle). Turn right on H Street, left on
New Hampshire Avenue, and right on Virginia Avenue. Cross Rock
Creek Parkway at crosswalk to reach parking lot of Thompson Boat
Center. Follow one-lane road over short bridge to waterfront.

DIREC-TIONS for the ride

- From Thompson's parking area, turn right onto bike path (Potomac River is on your right).
- Proceed 1.5 miles to Ericsson Monument. Turn left to head up short road (sign reads TAXIS ONLY) to Lincoln Memorial.
- Facing east toward the Capitol building, pick up bike path parallel to Reflecting Pool. Proceed 0.5 mile to Seventeenth Street pedestrian crossing (traffic signal).
- Take path short distance east (uphill) to Washington Monument. Proceed on bike/foot paths across Fifteenth and Fourteenth Streets to Jefferson Drive. Begin tour of south side of National Mall.
- Follow Jefferson Drive about 0.5 mile along Mall. Detour here for the shorter version. Otherwise, turn right on Third Street and quick left on Maryland Avenue. Proceed past statue of James Garfield to U.S. Capitol grounds.
- Follow footpaths around south side of Capitol building to east front. Proceed to East Capitol Street. Pass through stone gates; go left on First Street.
- If interested in the Capitol Hill detour, ride 1 block to East Capitol Street, turn right and pick up those directions. Otherwise, take First Street about 0.75 mile to Columbus Circle in front of Union Station. Turn right on circle and left onto service road in front of station. Watch out for traffic in this busy area.
- Exit station area on service road; turn left. Take second right on Louisiana Avenue.
- Proceed less than 1 mile past parks and bell tower. Take oblique right onto Constitution Avenue. In 2 blocks turn right onto Pennsylvania Avenue (heavy traffic except on weekends).
- In 11 blocks, turn right on Thirteenth Street and quick left on Pennsylvania Avenue North. Pass National Theater and Willard Hotel to reach Fifteenth Street. Cross at signal to continue straight on Hamilton Place. Walk bike on sidewalk.
- In about ½ block, turn right through the gates onto East Executive Avenue. Exit through another set of gates; turn left past the White House. Cross at Seventeenth Street signal and turn left.

- Ride 3 long blocks to Constitution Avenue. Cross at signal and pick up bike path (west) past Constitution Gardens and Vietnam Veterans Memorial.
- Return up Henry Bacon Drive to Lincoln Memorial. Return to Ericsson statue and retrace route to Thompson's.

North side of Mall elective: This route stays on the Mall and avoids some heavily-trafficked roads. It also shaves several miles from the trip while affording a chance to see the Mall's other four museums: the National Gallery (East Building and West Building, featuring dramatically different collections), the Museum of Natural History, and the Museum of American History, which features an interesting selection of antique bicycles—not to mention a seminude statue of George Washington.

Directions from Jefferson Drive:
- Left on Third Street.
- Left on Madison Drive (one way).
- Straight on to Fourteenth Street. Cross to Washington Monument grounds.
- Straight to Seventeenth Street. Cross to path parallel to Constitution Avenue.
- Follow signs to Constitution Gardens and Vietnam Veterans Memorial.
- Follow path to Lincoln Memorial.

Capitol Hill Detour: This 2-mile side trip through a Victorian row-house neighborhood takes you past the homes of many members of Congress. Be sure to stop at Eastern Market, an old-fashioned farmers' market at Seventh Street and North Carolina Avenue, for a late breakfast or lunch.

From east front of U.S. Capitol:
- Straight on East Capitol Street, 11 blocks to Lincoln Park.
- Turn right on Eleventh Street.
- In 1 block, turn right on North Carolina Avenue.

- After stopping at Eastern Market, proceed on North Carolina to Pennsylvania Avenue. Turn right.
- Left on Independence Avenue at Second Street. Take first right onto First Street. Proceed 5 long blocks to Union Station to pick up the route.

Pick up the path leading directly uphill to the Washington Monument, where a circle of flags always blows stiffly. This high ground is a favored spot for kite-flying. The cornerstone for the 555-foot-tall monument was laid in 1848, but the masonry structure was not completed until 1884. From 9:00 A.M. to 5:00 P.M. (until midnight in spring and summer), you can ride the elevator up to the 500-foot level (call ahead; in 1998 the Park Service began a multiyear renovation).

Back on your bike, continue downhill past a souvenir stand on a path to Fifteenth Street. Cross carefully and take another path to a signal at Fourteenth Street. Dismount and cross to one-way Jefferson Drive, the starting point for a tour of the south side of the National Mall. Conceived by Pierre L'Enfant as a residential boulevard, the Mall was densely planted as a romantic forest in the 1800s and streamlined as a grassy, elm-lined promenade in the early 1900s. It is the home of nine Smithsonian museums plus the National Gallery of Art, an ice-skating rink, and a building of the Department of Agriculture. All museums are free.

Your first stop is the recently renovated Freer Museum, the first Smithsonian art museum, dating from 1923. Housed in a building styled after an Italian palace, the Freer collection devotes itself to Asian art, particularly jade sculpture, lacquers, and porcelain. Not to be missed is the ornate Peacock Room, which was moved intact from art patron Charles Freer's Detroit mansion along with more than a hundred artworks by James Abbott McNeill Whistler.

The next few hundred feet feature:

• the turreted Smithsonian Castle, a romantic brownstone structure designed by the architect of St. Patrick's Cathedral;

• the Arts & Industries Building, a High Victorian pile exhibiting American technology as it existed in 1876;

• the doughnut-shaped Hirshhorn Museum and its outdoor sculpture garden, both devoted to modern art; and

• the National Air and Space Museum, which is the nation's most visited museum (9.5 million people annually). Within this great hangarlike structure you can find everything from the *Spirit of St. Louis* to space modules used in the Apollo-Soyuz project. Almost everyone takes in a 70-millimeter IMAX film, shown on the Langley Theater's five-story screen.

If you stop to dawdle at the Castle, don't miss the Smithsonian's newest museums: the National Museum of African Art and the Arthur M. Sackler Gallery, devoted to Asian art. Both are located beneath a landscaped plaza facing Independence Avenue.

If you are following the shorter, North side of Mall elective (recommended for those not comfortable cycling on urban streets), pick up those directions at this point. Continuing east, leave Jefferson Drive at Third Street to enter Maryland Avenue. On the right stands the U.S. Botanical Gardens, a Victorian-style greenhouse filled with tropical orchids and blooming cacti. Unless you take the shorter alternate route to see the Mall's north side (see "Directions for the ride" above), the next stop is what L'Enfant called "Congress House."

Started in 1793, burned in 1814, finished in 1867, and constantly updated since, the U.S. Capitol is situated on one of Washington's highest hills. In the 1870s it was landscaped by Frederick Law Olmsted, the principal designer of Manhattan's Central Park. The grounds retain odd little additions such as Japanese lanterns, a grotto, and a trolley stop. Follow a looping path to the Capitol's east side for views of the Library of Congress and the Supreme Court; then turn left on First Street. Follow First Street to where it intersects with East Capitol Street. You have the option to ride through the Capitol Hill neighborhood and visit a farmers' market at this point. If interested, turn right and pick up the directions for the Capitol Hill detour from here. Otherwise, continue straight on First Street and you will soon arrive at Union Station. Long empty and decaying, the 1907 station reopened in 1988 as a shopping mall after a painstaking $100 million restoration. Its Roman-inspired architecture matches that of just about any of D.C.'s great public buildings. Best of all, it still serves Amtrak, Metrorail, and commuter trains. Union Station features well-designed and well-located bike racks, so it's a good place to park the 18-speed and explore the city on foot or by rail.

After touring the grand station, exit the area via Louisiana Avenue, cutting diagonally southwest. Within 4 blocks, you'll meet Constitution Avenue. Turn right and in 2 blocks start cruising down the Avenue of the Presidents—Pennsylvania Avenue. Since the time of Thomas Jefferson, this 1-mile stretch has hosted the inaugural parade. Until recently, the street's seedy demeanor belied its importance. But a $1 billion effort since 1976 has resulted in four new parks and memorials, restoration of several major landmarks, and construction of new hotels, offices, and restaurants. On weekends the boulevard is lightly traveled. Don't miss the new Navy War Memorial, the Canadian Chancery, the National Archives, the FBI Building (open for a rat-a-tat of a tour), and the restored Old (1897) Post Office, with its 315-foot bell tower and pavilion filled with shops. At Thirteenth Street, Pennsylvania Avenue splits into North and South. Follow the ride directions until you reach a plaza anchored by a statue of Alexander Hamilton.

After 1 block, turn right through the gates onto East Executive Avenue, a landscaped lane flanking the White House. Walk your bike—there is always a crowd of people lining up for tours of the White House. Here an elaborate security system has been disguised to maintain the aesthetics of the grounds.

Passing through the gateway at the other end, turn left to arrive at 1600 Pennsylvania Avenue N.W., the address of every American president since John Adams. Designed by Irish-born architect James Hoban, the White House was painted its alabaster hue to cover damage caused by the British burning of 1814. Pennsylvania Avenue fronting the White House was closed to vehicular traffic in 1995. Drivers grumbled at the time, but walkers, joggers, in-line skaters, and cyclists have since turned this most famous stretch of street into a festive, car-free promenade.

Just past the White House on the right stands Blair-Lee House, a kind of guest house for the White House. You can usually tell who is visiting by the color of the flags flying. Next door is the Renwick Gallery, a Smithsonian museum devoted to objects made by Contemporary American artisans.

Carefully picking your way through one of Washington's busiest intersections, turn left on Seventeenth Street. Pass another fine art museum, the Corcoran Gallery, and the Organization of American States Building. Continue south to reach Constitution Avenue, a grand esplanade built on top of the old city canal. The last vestige of the canal, which was an open sewer as much as a waterway, is the old lockkeeper's house at Seventeenth and Constitution. Cross the road to find a winding path to the right to Constitution Gardens, a fifty-acre park dedicated in 1976. It features 5,000 trees, including honey locust, dogwood, and maple, and a seven-and-one-half-acre lake that is home to carp, turtles, mallards, and geese.

Follow signs to the Vietnam Veterans Memorial. Designed by twenty-one-year-old architecture student Maya Lin, who won an open competition, the memorial features the names of 58,000 soldiers inscribed on a wall of polished black granite. In 1993 the Vietnam Women's Memorial by sculptor Glenna Goodacre was added to honor the work of the women Vietnam veterans. Expect crowds, flowers, tears. Signs forbid you to bring your bike right up to "The Wall." Proceed up Henry Bacon Drive back to the Lincoln Memorial and double back to the Thompson Boat Center.

Rock Creek Park: D.C.

Distance:	9-mile loop
Approximate pedaling time:	1 hour
Terrain:	Rolling
Surface:	Paved multiuse trail, narrow at times
Things to see:	Oak Hill Cemetery, National Zoo, grist mill
Facilities:	Rest rooms at Zoo and Pierce Mill
Recommended for:	Tourists, Families with children, Natural beauty, Mostly bike paths

In 1863 the naturalist John Burroughs wrote, "There is perhaps not another city in the Union that has on its threshold so much natural beauty and grandeur, such as men seek for in remote forests and mountains. A few touches of art would convert this whole region into a park unequalled in the world." The area he referred to was north of settled Washington, a forested place full of glens and meadows and ferns.

A few years later, the U.S. Army Corps of Engineers surveyed the same area, seeking a healthful new site for the White House. Instead they recommended that Rock Creek would make an excellent city greensward. Finally, in 1890, Burroughs's wish came true when Congress created 1,800-acre Rock Creek Park in the Northwest quadrant.

Today this stream valley once inhabited by the Algonquins provides recreation for many of D.C.'s 570,000 residents. In addition to boulder-strewn Rock Creek, it contains several other streams, tennis courts, hiking and bridle trails, a nature center, planetarium, and historic buildings. The park provides an excellent commuting route for

Tilden St.

Pierce Mill
R

Connecticut Ave.

National Zoo R

Ellington Bridge

Taft Bridge

NORTH

Oak Hill
Cemetery

Rock Creek

GEORGETOWN

POTOMAC

Thompson Boat Center R
Park &
START

ROOSEVELT
ISLAND

VIRGINIA

RIVER

HOW
to get
there

From north, Rock Creek Parkway south to Thompson's parking lot; turn right. From Mall, Virginia Avenue west across Rock Creek Parkway to Thompson's parking lot. From Virginia, Theodore Roosevelt Bridge or Memorial Bridge to Rock Creek Parkway to Thompson's parking lot. By Metro, Blue or Orange Line to Foggy Bottom/GWU station, about 1 mile walk or ride. From Metro station, walk south on Twenty-third Street (away from Washington Circle). Turn right on H Street, left on New Hampshire Avenue, and right on Virginia Avenue. Cross Rock Creek Parkway at crosswalk to reach parking lot of Thompson Boat Center. Follow one-lane road over short bridge to waterfront.

DIREC-TIONS
for the ride

- From Thompson Boat Center cross one-lane short bridge to parking lot.
- From parking lot, take curb cut at left to join Rock Creek Trail.
- After passing exercise course, dismount and cross Rock Creek Parkway at crosswalk.
- Bear right at fork in trail and ride under arches of Ellington Bridge.
- At tunnel, turn left and ride through gate to path bordering Rock Creek.
- At service road crossing, turn left to ride over stone bridge into National Zoo.
- Return to trail via stone bridge. Turn left to head north.
- At parking lot near waterfall, turn left to visit Pierce Mill and Art Barn.
- Return to trail to join rides described in Ride 4, Ride 5, or Ride 11.
- To return to Thompson Boat Center, turn around and retrace steps.

bikers from the neighborhoods of Cleveland Park, Woodley Park, Mount Pleasant, and Adams-Morgan to downtown D.C.

The park also provides a sanctuary for more wildlife than one might expect in the heart of a city. Look for mallards, wood ducks, and even a family of black-crowned night herons in the creek. You may also spot raccoons, foxes, deer, and beaver nearby.

A tour of Rock Creek Park begins at the creek's mouth on the Potomac. You can rent a bike (or a canoe or rowing shell) at the Harry T. Thompson Boat Center just off Virginia Avenue and Rock Creek Parkway N.W. Thompson's (open March to November) also has bike racks, lockers, water fountains, and rest rooms.

Leaving Thompson's, with the Watergate Apartment complex and Kennedy Center on your right, turn left on the path heading north. Note on the right, on the other side of the Rock Creek Parkway and beneath a freeway ramp, the ruins of the Godey lime kiln, a vestige of

a prosperous nineteenth-century industry. The path winds along the Parkway for the next 3 miles, at times almost grazing the road and then disappearing into thickets of woods. It crosses Rock Creek five times on bridges.

An exercise course parallels the route. On a spring day, the path becomes an olio of humanity, with Lycra-clad runners and cyclists mingling with baby strollers, birders, and groups of Chinese from the nearby embassy of the People's Republic. You'll even see children fishing and wading in the creek. In spring the embankment blazes with thousands of jonquils, daffodils, and tulips, while the woods bloom with dogwoods and redbud. In addition to the bright shades of crimson and yellow provided by these flora, the park always seems cool, green, and mossy thanks to its many trees and rock formations. The boulders that turn Rock Creek into cascades and provide dramatic outcroppings in the valley are the same type of Potomac Bluestone carved into building stone for the visitor's center and handsomely crafted retaining walls within the park.

Passing under the decks of several old auto bridges, you pedal next to Oak Hill Cemetery, a twelve-acre burial ground founded in 1849 and filled with ornate Victorian monuments. As you pass under the Dumbarton Bridge, note the Indian heads carved in sandstone. This is also near the site of Lyons Mill, which was built in 1780 but collapsed with a roar in 1913. The stone piers for the bike-path bridge are all that remain of what was once Rock Creek's biggest industry.

After carefully crossing three parkway entrance ramps, you will thread under the Taft Bridge (1909) and then the Ellington Bridge (1935), named for jazz musician Duke Ellington and identifiable by three graceful arches rising 150 feet from the creek basin. Bear right on the path to travel under one of those arches. After crossing a small bridge with a narrow sidewalk, come to a parkway tunnel that contains an even slenderer path. Avoid the tunnel by turning left onto a smooth path parallel to Rock Creek. Glide over a stone bridge to the left to arrive at the National Zoological Park.

Founded in 1890 and laid out by Frederick Law Olmsted, the first landscape architect in the United States and designer of Central Park in New York City, the 163-acre zoo features hundreds of species of reptiles and mammals, including a giant panda and golden tamarind monkeys. Bicycle riding is not allowed in the zoo, but you can park your bike (locked securely!) or walk it to any of the nearby exhibits. Lately, the zoo has been developing what it calls "BioParks," which are realistic and edifying replicas of diverse ecosystems. In 1992 the zoo realized this concept by building Amazonia, a $12 million rain-forest exhibition under a climate-controlled dome.

Back on the trail, you wind along through hardwood forest and dense alder bushes for a mile or so (be sure to check the creek for wood ducks and kingfishers) until arriving at Pierce Mill, the last of eight water-powered mills once driven by Rock Creek.

Built about 1820 from blue granite, the mill was restored in 1985 by the National Park Service. You once could buy buckwheat and cornmeal ground on site through a remarkable system of millstones, wooden gears, shafts, hoppers, and chutes. However, the milling equipment broke in 1993; the Friends of Pierce Mill (8404 Pittsfield Court, Potomac, MD) are raising funds in hopes of restoring it to working order. Close by are picnic grounds, rest rooms, and the Art Barn, a gallery installed in a former carriage house.

Continue north to the Pierce Mill parking lot. On weekends and holidays, this is the starting place for an exhilarating 10-mile round-trip on Beach Drive, closed to traffic. But on weekdays, the road reverts to a major commuter byway, and though it is marked an on-road bike path, I don't recommend it. If you're making this tour on a weekday, return to Thompson's the way you came. The remainder of Rock Creek Park is a treat best saved for weekends. To add about 8 miles, combine this ride with Ride 11 (Upper Reaches of Rock Creek Park).

On the trip back, the first bridge you traverse is a concrete span stamped 1982. Look to the left across the road to view a bench carved from granite and inscribed JUSSERAND—PERSONAL TRIBUTE OF ESTEEM AND AFFECTION—1855–1932. (Jusserand was a French ambassador and friend of Teddy Roosevelt.)

Rock Creek Park
D.C. to Maryland and Back

Distance:	27-mile loop
Approximate pedaling time:	2–3 hours
Terrain:	Rolling
Surface:	Smooth roads closed to cars weekends and holidays, on-road routes, and paved off-road paths
Things to see:	Ravines of upper Rock Creek, Walter Reed Annex, Mormon Temple and gardens, Kensington antiques center, Woodend estate, Miller Cabin, Pierce Mill
Facilities:	Rest rooms at Pierce Mill, Park Service Substation, and Meadowbrook Park; food and antiques shops in Kensington; gift shop at Woodend
Options:	2.4-mile round-trip to Walter Reed Annex; 2.8-mile round-trip to historic Kensington
Recommended for:	Tourists, families with children (only on weekends), Natural beauty, Mostly bike paths

In the 1970s the National Park Service agreed to a bold experiment. On weekends and holidays, Beach Drive, one of the busiest roads leading into Rock Creek Park, would be closed to motorized traffic.

Perhaps to the pleasant surprise of the men in green, park use actually increased on auto-free days. So the Park Service institutionalized 7:00 A.M. to 7:00 P.M. closings of portions of the road. Meanwhile,

KENSINGTON

R Viers Mill
• Historic R.R. Arch

Beach Dr.
(Parallel Bike Path)

R
Kensington Pkway.

Mormon Temple

Stoneybrook Rd.

Pagoda
Walter Reed Annex

Georgetown Branch Bike Trail

Woodend
R

Jones Mill Rd.

East-West Highway

Meadowbrook Park R

D.C.

NORTH

MARYLAND

Connecticut Ave.

Beach Dr.

Miller Cabin

Park Service Station R

Beach Dr.

Park &
START ★ • Pierce Mill R

HOW to get there Heading south on Connecticut Avenue, turn left on Tilden Street to Pierce Mill parking lot. From Rock Creek Parkway, head north to Tilden Street, turn left to Pierce Mill parking lot. From Sixteenth Street, take Piney Branch Parkway west to Pierce Mill parking lot. By Metro, take Red Line to Cleveland Park station, then ride 0.25 mile to Tilden Street; turn right to Pierce Mill parking lot.

DIREC-TIONS for the ride

- From Pierce Mill parking area, head north on path, with creek to your right.
- Pass through auto barriers (weekends only) to enter Beach Drive.
- Stay on Beach Drive north past D.C. line. Follow bike route signs, turning right over a narrow wooden bridge at Meadowbrook Park, then left around the park and past the Meadowbrook stables.
- Cross East-West Highway at traffic light to pick up off-road trail. Bear right where the Georgetown Branch Trail intersects with the bike path. (Ride 5 may be picked up at this point.)
- Pass small playground; then take optional right turn up zigzag path to Walter Reed Annex.
- Stay on path to Kensington Parkway (four-way stop). Turn right for detour to Kensington.
- Return to path and turn right. Continue to Viers Mill and turn around. (*Option:* Continue 5 miles north to Lake Needwood.)
- To return on road, turn left onto Beach Drive.
- Pass Mormon Temple; then right on unmarked Jones Mill Road.
- Watch for Woodend sign; right on steep drive to explore estate.
- Return to Jones Mill. At intersection with Jones Bridge Road, continue straight. Note the Georgetown Branch Trail connection just 20 yards past the intersection. Continue down Jones Mill Road, which turns into Beach Drive after the East-West Highway intersection.
- Beach Drive back to Pierce Mill.

an off-road trail was paved through the 2,700-acre Maryland section of Rock Creek Regional Park, providing an uninterrupted 12.5-mile ride from Pierce Mill in D.C. to Viers Mill in Maryland. The trail also extends 5 miles farther north to Lake Needwood, where pedalboats and canoes may be rented in summertime.

This route is organized as a round-trip combining pathway and roadway travel. If you are nervous about cars, stick to the paths, but expect competition from strollers and pets.

The northern D.C. section of Rock Creek is flat-out gorgeous. Riding along a two-lane parkway designed to provide great vistas of hardwood forests and rushing waters, you can easily imagine yourself a hundred miles from the city.

After crossing East-West Highway, pick up an off-road trail that leads you under the remains of an old Baltimore & Ohio train trestle and through wetlands and stands of evergreens. Bear right where the Georgetown Branch Trail intersects. After passing a small playground, turn right to detour uphill on an old footpath to the Walter Reed Army Medical Center Annex, a fascinating and eccentric campus on a high hill.

Built as a women's seminary nearly a century ago and annexed by the army during World War II, the 190-acre complex is almost like a pop-up sampler of world architecture. There's a Japanese pagoda, a Dutch windmill, a 600-year-old Roman fountain, a Bavarian resort hotel with stained-glass windows, and dormitory buildings that wouldn't look out of place in seventeenth-century Brussels. The idea was to provide the female seminarians with the sophistication afforded by world travel without exposing them to worldly evils. Unfortunately, the army says the badly deteriorating buildings will be torn down. Although preservationists promise a spirited fight, I wouldn't wait too long to see this architectural oddity. (For more information, contact Save Our Seminary at Forest Glen, P.O. Box 8274, Silver Spring, MD 20907, or check the Web site at http://www. operant.com/Seminary.

The next point of interest, accessible from Stoneybrook Road, is the Washington Temple for the Church of Jesus Christ of the Latter-Day Saints. Soaring upright from a field of electric-green grass, the temple's profile from afar has been compared to Dorothy's first sighting of Oz. One of forty-one Mormon temples worldwide reserved for sacred ceremonies such as marriages and baptisms, the gleaming structure of white Alabama marble was completed in 1974. It rises 288 feet to a gold-plated statue of the angel Moroni. The temple is closed to non-Mormons, but you can see photos of the sanctum sanctorum in the visitor's center. The fifty-six-acre grounds are also worth a look.

Back on the trail, head west parallel to the creek through residential neighborhoods. At a four-way stop take a right on Kensington Parkway to visit the town of Kensington, a Victorian streetcar suburb with grand old frame houses and many antiques shops. After taking tea at the Country Cupboard Tea Room (3750 Howard Avenue), return to the path to head north to Viers Mill, a county park.

Ride back to D.C. on Jones Mill Road and Beach Drive for different scenery and sights. This route affords a chance to see Woodend, the headquarters of the Audubon Naturalist Society of the Central Atlantic States. The forty-acre estate is cultivated to provide a variety of habitats that have attracted rabbits, bullfrogs, woodpeckers, and even wild turkeys to the midst of this suburban area. There's also a formal garden and a Georgian mansion, which contains a shop selling books, calendars, binoculars, toys, and bird feeders. I find this shop particularly useful before Christmas. While the rest of Washington fumes in shopping traffic, I'm playing Santa with spokes, pedaling off to Woodend to stuff my panniers with gifts. Look closely for Woodend's small sign—it's easy to miss.

Back on a narrow, winding road lined with bungalows, you soon come to an intersection with Jones Bridge Road. About 20 yards past the intersection is the Georgetown Branch Trail. This disused freight line is part of what local hikers and bikers hope will become a fully paved, 11-mile path linking Silver Spring, Maryland, with Georgetown and the C & O Canal National Historical Park. The stretch here is part of the hard-packed gravel path between Silver Spring and Bethesda; it connects with the paved Capital Crescent Trail, which runs between Bethesda and Georgetown. See Ride 5 for a very pleasant loop using these connected bike trails and Rock Creek Park. The stretch from Georgetown to downtown Bethesda is complete. It's at the heart of this book's next ride, "Capital Crescent Loop."

The return to Pierce Mill via Beach Drive is almost all downhill. Keep an eye out for crow-sized pileated woodpeckers attacking the hardwood trees lining this winding road. Also, several miles down Beach Drive, take a look at the former home of Joaquin Miller, the "Poet of the Sierras," who lived in Washington in the 1880s. Located on the west side of Beach Drive, it is reputed to be the only log cabin in D.C. The Miller Cabin hosts poetry readings on many summer nights.

Capital Crescent Loop

Distance:	22 miles
Approximate pedaling time:	3 hours
Terrain:	Flat
Surface:	Paved recreational trails and gravel bike paths
Things to see:	Area's newest rail-to-trail conversion project, the C & O Canal, a bit of downtown Bethesda, old Chevy Chase houses, Rock Creek Park
Recommended for:	Tourists (on weekends), Families with children, Natural beauty, Mostly bike paths

Over the past decade or so, hundreds of communities across the country have turned abandoned railroad rights-of-way into attractive multiuse trails and linear parks. These "rail-to-trail" conversions have proved hugely popular. Their gentle grade makes them ideal for walking, jogging, in-line skating, cycling, and more.

At last count there were nearly 1,000 completed rail-trails, totaling over 10,000 miles in every state of the union, as well as Washington, D.C. They range in length from a few miles to a few hundred miles.

The Washington area joined the movement in a big way in the 1980s with the completion of the 45-mile long W & OD Trail from Arlington to the town of Purcellville, in the shadow of the Blue Ridge Mountains (see this book's next ride for complete details). Then came the 12-mile WB & A Trail in Prince George's and Anne Arundel Counties.

Now, with the completion of its initial 7-mile stretch from the

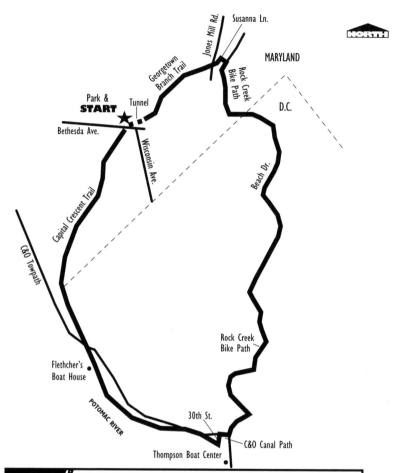

Susanna Ln.

Jones Mill Rd.

Georgetown Branch Trail

Rock Creek Bike Path

MARYLAND

D.C.

Park & **START**

Tunnel

Bethesda Ave.

Wisconsin Ave.

Beach Dr.

Capital Crescent Trail

C&O Towpath

Rock Creek Bike Path

Flethcher's Boat House

POTOMAC RIVER

30th St.

C&O Canal Path

Thompson Boat Center

NORTH

HOW to get there

Start at the public parking lot at the corner of Bethesda and Woodmont Avenues in Bethesda. From downtown D.C., follow Wisconsin Avenue to Bethesda, then turn left on Leland Street to Woodmont and Bethesda Avenues. From the direction of Rockville, follow Wisconsin Avenue into town, then turn right onto Woodmont just past the National Institutes of Health and continue to Bethesda Avenue. Or, take the Metro to the Bethesda station on the Red Line. Exit via the Metro elevator onto Wisconsin Avenue, follow Wisconsin Avenue south for 3 blocks to Bethesda Avenue, then turn right for 2 blocks to Woodmont.

DIREC-TIONS for the ride

- From the entrance to the Capital Crescent Trail on Bethesda Avenue, turn right and cross Woodmont Avenue.
- Turn left onto bike path leading to a tunnel under Wisconsin Avenue.
- At end of tunnel, hard-packed gravel marks the start of the Georgetown Branch Trail.
- Follow the trail past the golf course. Cross Connecticut Avenue and ride on the sidewalk to reach the bike trail.
- Cross Jones Bridge Road, make a quick left and right onto Susanna Lane. Follow the road around to the left and back onto the bike path.
- Shortly, the Georgetown Branch Trail will intersect with the Rock Creek Trail. Turn right on the Rock Creek Trail, toward downtown Washington, D.C.
- Continue straight on the Rock Creek Trail where the Georgetown Branch Trail goes off to the left at a small playground.
- Cross East-West Highway onto Meadowbrook Lane. Keeping the stables on your right, turn right toward Meadowbrook Park.
- At the park, turn right over a small bridge, then left onto Beach Drive.
- Follow the Rock Creek bike path toward Georgetown. (See Ride 3 for details.)
- Pass under M Street and Pennsylvania Avenue overpasses.
- Fifty yards after riding beneath overpasses, turn right onto a brick path leading into the C & O Canal National Historic Park. Follow it 2 blocks and turn left on 30th Street. You've missed it if you reach Thompson Boat House in another hundred yards.
- Turn right on K Street under the Whitehurst Freeway. Ride the full length of K Street to the beginning of the Capital Crescent Trail.
- Follow the Capital Crescent Trail for its entire length back to Bethesda. Along the way, you'll ride alongside the C & O Canal before crossing a bridge over it; pass through a tunnel beneath

MacArthur Boulevard; cross a bridge over Massachusetts Avenue; and cross Little Falls Parkway.

■ Reach the Trail's end at Bethesda Avenue.

---

heart of Georgetown to downtown Bethesda, the Capital Crescent Trail joins the list. Although relatively short, it boasts Potomac River views, a restored trestle bridge over the C & O Canal, and a brick-vaulted railroad tunnel. It also offers a completely car-free commuting route from Bethesda to downtown. And for longer rides it features direct connections to the C & O towpath (Ride 14), Rock Creek Park (Ride 4), and Virginia's extensive trail system (Rides 1, 15, and 16).

This ride connects the paved Capital Crescent Trail the gravel Georgetown Branch Trail, and Rock Creek Park. The resulting loop is high on fun, short on cars, and lacking in noticeable hills. The full loop is best on weekends when Beach Drive in Rock Creek Park is closed to traffic.

Start in downtown Bethesda, at the corner of Woodmont and Bethesda Avenues. Look for the entrance to the Capital Crescent Trail between the public parking lot on the corner and the car dealership on Bethesda Avenue. A natural foods market, two bagel stores, and a gourmet coffee shop—all within yards of the trailhead—offer an opportunity to fuel up for your ride. In the spirit of saving the best for last, though, ride away from the trail, following Bethesda Avenue to a tunnel under Wisconsin Avenue and onto the Georgetown Branch Trail.

The Georgetown Branch Trail winds through Chevy Chase, one of Washington's classic old neighborhoods. After passing older bungalows and colonial-style homes, you'll ride through the Chevy Chase Country Club. Proper etiquette demands that everyone—including riders—be quiet when golfers are putting.

For now, the Georgetown Branch Trail is hard-packed gravel. This bike path is planned to become part of the paved Capital Crescent Trail linking Georgetown with Silver Spring, Maryland. Follow the

Georgetown Branch Trail until it intersects with the Rock Creek Trail, then take that trail back into downtown Washington. (See Ride 3 for complete details on this stretch.)

Now comes the only tricky part. Just after crossing beneath the M Street and Pennsylvania Avenue overpasses, turn right onto the brick path leading into the C & O Canal National Historic Park. (You've gone too far if you reach Thompson Boat House on the right in another hundred yards.) Ride along the canal for 2 blocks, then turn left on 30th Street down to K Street, which runs under the Whitehurst Freeway. Turn right on K Street, and ride the length of K Street, passing the Washington Harbor development and the rest of Georgetown's waterfront on the left. At the very end, where K Street ends, the Capital Crescent Trail begins.

This trail (paved in 1995) traces the east bank of the Potomac River for a few miles before turning inland toward Bethesda. The views are best in fall or early spring, before thick growth turns it into a tunnel of greenery. You'll ride alongside the C & O Canal towpath for a short stretch. Fletcher's Boat House is on the left, where you can rent rowboats and one-speed bicycles (202–244–0461). The trail then curves right, crossing a restored railroad trestle bridge over the canal. Be sure to rest here for the view.

The trail's approximate midway point is marked by a cavernous, brick-vaulted tunnel beneath MacArthur Boulevard. The Bethesda public swimming pool at Little Falls Road will seem particularly welcoming on a hot summer day. (Be sure to pack a bathing suit, towel, and about $10 per person for snacks and entrance fees.) From there, it's just another 0.5 mile to the trail's end at Bethesda Avenue.

The W & OD Trail
Through Virginia Countryside

Distance:	39 miles, one way
Approximate pedaling time:	4 hours
Terrain:	Mostly flat and straight
Surface:	Paved multiuse trail
Things to see:	Historic train stations, farms, creeks, downtown Leesburg historic district
Facilities:	Rest rooms, restaurants, bike shops, country stores en route
Recommended for:	Families with children, Natural beauty, Mostly bikepaths, Countryside

The Washington and Old Dominion Railroad never was very success-ful. Founded in 1847 to connect towns on the Potomac to resort towns in the Blue Ridge Mountains, the rail line locals dubbed the "Virginia Creeper" ran sporadically and lost money for more than a century until closing for good in 1968.

Today, however, the W & OD line is a stunning success. Its 100-foot-wide right-of-way has been converted to a park stretching from the Arlington/Alexandria border to the rural town of Purcellville, 45 miles away. The Northern Virginia Regional Park Authority has cre-ated one of the most convenient, safe, and interesting trails in the capital region. You can easily reach the W & OD by Metrorail, super-highway, or other off-road trails (see Ride 15 for a connecting route). From Vienna to Purcellville, the wide, paved trail is augmented by a separate 30-mile gravel bridle path. The Park Authority constructed or restored seventeen bridges to whisk cyclists over stream beds and busy roads.

Dozens of roads and parking lots connect to the W & OD, so you

PURCELLVILLE
LEESBURG
R

VIRGINIA

15

POTOMAC RIVER

ASHBURN

HERNDON
R

RESTON

Dulles Toll Rd.

RESTON
TOWN CENTER

R

Gallows Rd.

VIENNA
R

Falls Church
★ Park &
START

ALEXANDRIA

NORTH

HOW to get there By auto, Interstate 66 or 495 to East Falls Church; park at Metro station. By Metro, Orange Line to East Falls Church Station. By bike, Interstate 66 bike trail, which stretches from Key Bridge in Rosslyn to merge with W & OD Trail (see description in Ride 15).

DIREC-TIONS for the ride

- From East Falls Church Metrorail station, turn right on Sycamore Street.
- Turn right on W & OD Trail to head toward Purcellville. Trail is well marked.
- Turn left on W & OD Trail to head toward Arlington. Trail is well marked.

can pick a starting point at will. One of the most popular is the Metrorail station in East Falls Church, from where you will encounter only a few miles of suburbia before getting to the "good stuff." Falls Church and Vienna, the next town along the trail, have interesting historic areas. In particular, the old train depot in Vienna now houses an elaborate model train operated by the Northern Virginia Model Railroaders Association. Traversing these towns does require some tedious crossings of busy roads and shopping plazas.

For a shorter ride that skips this suburban stretch, begin near the 17-mile marker in the planned community of Reston. Reston was founded in 1963 by Robert E. Simon, who envisioned a utopian community of mixed ages and income levels. Until recently, most of Reston looked like typical suburbia, but the new Reston Town Center has brought some urban splash. Located smack up against the W & OD, the eighty-five-acre area tries to re-create an open-air, lively city neighborhood: brick sidewalks, outdoor cafes, sixty shops of the BenneGapLimited variety, movie theaters, linden trees lined up along the streets, and a European-style central fountain. In keeping with the haute boutique atmosphere, there's a fancy bike shop that features a granite waterfall, polished hardwood floors—and bike rentals. A few miles ahead, the old burgs of Herndon and Sterling have retained their neat town centers. Farther west, the cyclist encounters open fields and picturesque streams, beginning with Broad Run.

The scenery is now divided between broad vistas and low gullies lined by thick underbrush. More than 450 wildflower species grow

along the W & OD, including Virginia Creeper, a vine with berries and five-pronged leaves. After passing an old quarry, you come to the country town of Ashburn. Be sure to stop at Partlow's Store, where you can buy anything from bananas to wading boots. The friendly dog on the porch *will* try to steal your granola bars.

Ride over an old railroad bridge over Goose Creek, and soon you're on the outskirts of Leesburg, seat of Loudoun County. Turn right on Catoctin Circle and right again on Market Street for a look at the old courthouse and the narrow streets of the historic district. The town was first named Georgetown after the king, and renamed in the 1700s for Thomas Lee, a wily planter and trader who excelled at Indian negotiations.

Leesburg was a Civil War site of minor importance. In an effort to dislodge Confederate troops in 1861, Union forces invaded the town via the 100-foot cliffs of Ball's Bluff. They were spectacularly rebuffed and suffered 1,700 casualties. An apocryphal tale has it that corpses of the blue brigade washed up 40 miles downriver in Washington's commercial district.

The W & OD runs another 9 miles west through rolling Loudoun County, ending in the old town of Purcellville. If the Park Authority reaches its goal of extending the trail a few miles more to Bluemont, they will have effected a connection to the 2,100-mile Appalachian Trail for hiking. In 1987 the U.S. Department of the Interior designated the whole park as a National Recreation Trail.

If you're interested in exploring the W & OD thoroughly, look for the fifty-six page *W & OD Trail Guide* at local bike shops or Northern Virginia Regional Parks offices. Or call the W & OD Trail office at (703) 729–0596 to order a copy. For a really long ride, this route connects with Rides 26 and 31.

Mount Vernon Trail
to Old Town Alexandria

Distance:	22-mile loop
Approximate pedaling time:	2–3 hours
Terrain:	Flat
Surface:	Smooth off-road trails and some busy roads
Things to see:	Jefferson Memorial, Reagan National Airport, sailing marina, historic Alexandria, Hunting Creek wildlife area
Facilities:	Rest rooms, snack bar, and bike shop at Daingerfield Island Marina
Recommended for:	Tourists, Families with children, Natural beauty, Mostly bike paths

On Sunday mornings, I often slip away to points usually too crowded to enjoy intimately. My avenue for this furtive endeavor is the Mount Vernon Trail, an 18.5-mile off-road path that links Washington with the estate of the president for whom the city was named. In between lies historic Alexandria, Virginia, a minor port in colonial America and a major tourist attraction today.

The trail parallels the George Washington Memorial Parkway, a scenic road built in 1932 for the bicentennial of the first president's birth. This ride begins at Harry T. Thompson Boat Center in Washington. (Turn to the end of this chapter for an alternative starting point at Theodore Roosevelt Island on the Virginia side.) Leaving Thompson's, turn right onto a path. As described in Ride 1, proceed to the Jefferson Memorial and cross the Fourteenth Street Bridge bike path to Virginia. At the end of the bridge, bear right onto a short

Park &
START
Thompson Boat Center ℞
Rock Creek Bike Path
1909 Bridge
Jefferson Memorial

Optional Park &
START

ROOSEVELT
ISLAND ℞

Memorial Bridge

14th St. Bridge

Reagan National
Airport

Marina
℞

ANACOSTIA RIVER

D.C.

VIRGINIA

NORTH

Mt. Vernon Trail

POTOMAC RIVER

Queen St.

Metro
Yellow Line

Royal St.

Union St.

King St.

OLD TOWN
ALEXANDRIA

MARYLAND

Jones Pt. Rd.

Hunting Creek

HOW to get there
From north, Rock Creek Parkway to Thompson's parking lot; turn right. From the Mall, Virginia Avenue west across Rock Creek Parkway to Thompson's parking lot. From Virginia, Roosevelt Bridge or Memorial Bridge to Rock Creek Parkway to Thompson's. By Metro, Blue or Orange Line to Foggy Bottom/GWU, about a 1-mile walk or ride. From Metro station, walk south on Twenty-third Street (away from Washington Circle). Turn right on H Street, left on New Hampshire Avenue, and right on Virginia Avenue. Cross Rock Creek Parkway at crosswalk to reach parking lot of Thompson Boat Center. Follow one-lane road over short bridge to waterfront.

DIREC- TIONS for the ride

- From Thompson Boat Center, right on bike path toward Watergate Apartments and Kennedy Center, Potomac River on right.
- Cross parkway intersection to reach path continuing between volleyball courts.
- Ride or walk through two short bridge underpasses.
- Straight through traffic circle at Ericsson Monument to Ohio Drive.
- Straight on Ohio Drive past soccer fields to cross 1909 bridge. Left at circular garden.
- Across from Jefferson Memorial entrance, right at curb cut to reach bikeway over Fourteenth Street Bridge.
- Cross bridge and bear right on bike path down to river level. Turn right onto Mount Vernon Trail, heading downriver.
- Follow trail signs past Reagan National Airport and sailing marina.
- In 4 miles, cross railroad tracks. Trail continues on North Union Street in Old Town Alexandria.
- Follow North Union to end of street onto off-road bike path. Path rejoins Jones Point Road parallel to Interstate 95.
- Turn left to visit historic Jones Point lighthouse. Retrace route and continue on Jones Point Road.
- Follow on-road path to Hunting Towers apartment complex at Washington Street. Left on sidewalk.
- Turn around at Hunting Creek Bridge. Retrace steps; bear left on Royal Street, on-road bike route through upper Old Town.
- Right on Queen Street. Left on Union to rejoin Mount Vernon route.
- Straight on Mount Vernon Trail past Navy and Marine Memorial and Lady Bird Johnson Park.
- To reach Memorial Bridge, bear left at the fork in trail and cross George Washington Parkway three times at crosswalks marked with stripes.
- Using Memorial Bridge sidewalk, cross to D.C. to Lincoln Memorial.

- Take unmarked path back to Ericsson Monument and retrace path back to Thompson's.

---

stretch of path that drops down to river level. Turn right onto the Mount Vernon Trail, heading downriver.

Passing a soccer field on the right, come to Gravelly Point, a good place to see the monuments—and landing jets—in profile. Continue through a parking lot to traverse Reagan National Airport. This part isn't the most scenic ride in the world, but it's not without interest. Much of the 750-acre airport was built in the 1930s under WPA programs, and the original buildings retain some of their streamlined, New Deal charm. In 1997, a mammoth new main terminal was dedicated. In 1998, on the eve of his 87th birthday, the airport was named for former president Ronald Reagan. Carefully cross four parkway ramps to reach the marina at Daingerfield Island. On any given day, this windswept spit attracts hundreds of sailors, sunbathers, and windsurfers. You will also find a snack bar, bike shop, restaurant, and rest rooms. Bike and boat rentals are available at the marina. For information call (703) 548–9027.

Now head south through a marsh full of cattails. Keep an eye out for circling hawks. When the path comes to a fork, bear left for a ride *above* the Potomac. To get around the area's industrial property, the Park Service built a cantilevered trail protruding from a retaining wall and supported by diagonal steel struts. The scenery is now a mixture of new office parks, an old rail line, Potomac vistas, and Alexandria's network of waterfront parks. Take a short detour through the Canal Square office complex to view a most unusual fountain. After crossing the railroad bed, graded flush with the road, reach North Union Street, heading for Alexandria's historic heart.

Founded by Scottish immigrants and laid out in 1749 with help from surveyor George Washington, Alexandria grew into a thriving tobacco port. In 1791 the burg was incorporated into the nascent District of Columbia. Town leaders agitated successfully for a return to mother Virginia in 1846. Alexandria escaped destruction during the Civil War, thereby retaining a large collection of brick and gingerbread houses of all eras.

It's easy to roam the gridiron of 200 city blocks by bicycle. Particularly worthwhile are Queen and Prince Streets (perpendicular to the river), and Royal and St. Aspaph Streets (parallel to the waterfront). The city's housing trademark is the oblong "flounder house," whose side porch looks like it should face front. King Street hums with bookshops, pubs, and restaurants. Heading uphill, it leads to the 330-foot-tall George Washington Masonic Memorial, the area's second-tallest building after the Washington Monument.

Be sure to visit historic Christ Church, attended by both George Washington and Robert E. Lee; the Lyceum, a history museum; and the Torpedo Factory, a World War I munitions plant that now houses 200 artists' studios. There's a visitor's center at 221 King Street.

Back on your two-wheeler, head south on North Union Street. Follow bike-path signs until you reach the end of North Union where the bike path continues through a wooded area to Jones Point, the site of an old whitewashed lighthouse marking the city's original southern tip. After visiting the lighthouse, retrace your steps, and follow the bike path signs until you reach busy Washington Street. The route continues on a sidewalk. In a few hundred feet stop at a stone bridge and pull out your lightweight binoculars. Among tidal flats and rotting piers, you can spot snowy egrets, hooded mergansers, and bufflehead ducks, not to mention eagles and falcons.

Rather than moving on to Mount Vernon—the route there from Alexandria is covered in the next chapter—turn around for a slightly different return to Washington. Follow the alternate bike route on Royal Street, a typical Old Town lane with narrow row houses. Turn left on King Street to visit the Masonic Memorial, or catch Metrorail's Yellow Line back to downtown D.C. Otherwise, head north to Queen Street, turn right, and rejoin the bike path at Founders Park on the waterfront.

In 4 miles, bypass the Fourteenth Street Bridge and keep straight. Pass the Lady Bird Johnson Park and bear left where the path continues under Memorial Bridge. Cross the George Washington Parkway and follow the bike path over three roads and onto the sidewalk of Memorial Bridge. Off to the left you can see eighty-eight-acre Theodore Roosevelt Island, once a country estate and now a park. Follow the bike route past the Lincoln Memorial and back to Thompson's.

To shorten this ride and skip its two crossings over the Potomac River, start at Theodore Roosevelt Island on the Virginia side. Park in the lot just off the George Washington Memorial Parkway. Ride south on the new boardwalk/asphalt path to connect with the Mount Vernon Trail. When you return, take the time to explore at least some of the island's 2.5 miles of trails and its memorial plaza.

Mount Vernon Trail
Alexandria to Mount Vernon

Distance:	18-mile loop
Approximate pedaling time:	2 hours
Terrain:	Rolling
Surface:	Smooth off-road trails and boardwalks
Things to see:	Old Town Alexandria, Dyke Marsh, Fort Hunt Park, Riverside Park, Mount Vernon
Facilities:	Rest rooms at parks, food and souvenirs at Mount Vernon
Options:	6-mile trip to Woodlawn Plantation; Fort Hunt Park
Recommended for:	Tourists, Families with children, Natural beauty, Bike paths

The final 8-mile leg of the Mount Vernon Trail resembles a trip to a country estate. It is far more bucolic than the first section. The terrain is also more undulating, which provides some Potomac views.

Start in Old Town Alexandria at the King Street Metrorail station. You can either arrive by Metro during valid hours for bike passes (see Appendix) or park at the station. Head away from the station on King Street, which is lined with antiques stores and pubs. In 1 mile turn right on Union Street to join the Mount Vernon Trail.

As described in Ride 7, follow signs to Hunting Creek, then continue straight, with a marshy area of the Potomac due left. You will soon arrive at two parks. The first, Belle Haven, indeed provides respite for sailors, picnickers, and bird-watchers. In season you can rent small sailboats here. Next door stands Dyke Marsh, a 240-acre wildlife preserve rescued from an earlier life as a gravel pit. If it's not muddy, ride out on a spit that juts into the Potomac for a look at this sprawling cat-

D.C.

ANACOSTIA RIVER

VIRGINIA

POTOMAC RIVER

D.C.

NORTH

(Yellow Line)

King St.

★ Park &
START

Union St.

R

MARYLAND

ALEXANDRIA

Mt. Vernon Trail

Dyke
Marsh

Woodlawn
Plantation
R

Fort Hunt
Park

Traffic Circle

Mt. Vernon
R

HOW
to get
there

By Metro, Yellow Line to King Street in Alexandria. By car,
George Washington Memorial Parkway south to Washington Street; turn right on King Street and drive 1 mile to Metro
parking lot, or continue straight 3 miles to Belle Haven/Dyke
Marsh parking. By bike, combine with route described in Ride 7.

DIREC-TIONS for the ride

- Start in Alexandria at King Street Metro or Belle Haven picnic area (the latter cuts about 3 miles from trip).
- From King Street, ride east 1 mile to Union Street. Turn right.
- Follow bike-path signs to Hunting Towers apartments on Washington Street. Bear left on sidewalk, which turns into bike path again shortly.
- Follow bike-path signs to Mount Vernon, with optional side trips to Dyke Marsh (1-mile round-trip on dirt path) and Fort Hunt Park (1-mile loop on park road).
- Retrace path back to starting point.

Option: At Mount Vernon, ride around the traffic circle and head west on Mount Vernon Highway. Off-road bike path is available, but on-road shoulder is fairly wide and flat. In 3 miles, carefully cross Route 1 to enter Woodlawn Plantation.

tail marsh. In spring the sanctuary hosts 250 bird species, not to mention wild iris, muskrats, frogs, and turtles. It's a glimpse of what these banks looked like two centuries ago.

Back on the route to Mount Vernon, the trail continues on a boardwalk through the marsh. There's a bench for pausing and pondering. Last time there I was treated to a five-minute dogfight as a fish hawk, its talons flaring, buzzed any herons and hawks that dared enter its territory.

Soon the path becomes more winding as hardwood forest closes in. After crossing a bridge across the parkway—noting the handsome construction of the stone span—glide downhill on a grassy median planted with blooming trees and evergreens, then climb again up to a bluff with fine views. The stone structure across the river is Fort Washington, a star-shaped fortress designed by Washington planner Pierre L'Enfant. Coast down to Fort Hunt Park, which has its own military ruins among 156 acres of picnic grounds.

Other sites worth visiting along the path include River Farm, a former holding of George Washington that is now the headquarters of the American Horticultural Society (public welcome to tour gardens and picnic on the river) and Riverside Park, a picnic area on a mini-spit of land next to Little Hunting Creek, just before the approach to Mount Vernon.

The remainder of the trail stays close to inlets and bays of the river until it jinks to the right and then climbs, signaling the approach to the estate of George and Martha Washington. Located on high ground on a bend in the river, the crescent-shaped house is surprisingly small but faultlessly elegant. Its Georgian facade was designed to fool the eye. It resembles sandstone but, when tapped, resounds with a knock. To simulate more expensive material, the colonials molded wood into masonrylike blocks and mixed sand with the paint for a rough finish.

The grounds also feature winding paths, formal gardens, trees planted by the general himself, and outbuildings filled with colonial tools and carriages. The estate is lovingly maintained and interpreted by the Mount Vernon Ladies' Association, which also provides tours. In 1858 the group rescued Mount Vernon from ruin, thereby launching the American historic preservation movement—and making possible the survival of many other sites noted in this book.

Leaving Mount Vernon, carefully cross a traffic circle for an optional 6-mile round-trip to another site associated with Washington. The Mount Vernon Highway leads to Woodlawn Plantation, once home to Washington's adopted daughter, Nelly Custis Lewis. It's now a house museum run by the National Trust for Historic Preservation. Here the Garden Club of Virginia carefully tends thirty-six rose beds hedged by dwarf species of English boxwood. Also on the grounds is a Frank Lloyd Wright house, which the National Trust rescued from a highway's path and moved to Woodlawn in the 1950s.

Rosemont Ramble

Distance:	8 miles
Approximate pedaling time:	90 minutes
Terrain:	Flat with one climb
Surface:	Good suburban roads and on-road bike lanes
Things to see:	Torpedo Factory, shops of King Street, The Lyceum, Gentry Row, George Washington Masonic Memorial, neighborhoods of Rosemont and Del Ray
Facilities:	Shops, rest rooms, Metrorail stop
Recommended for:	Tourists

This is a sightseeing figure eight of Alexandria that shows off both eighteenth-century Old Town and late-nineteenth-century historic neighborhoods. It is easily reached by Metro or bike paths from D.C.

Start at the King Street Metrorail station about 1 mile west of the Potomac River. The main landmark is a big one: the 330-foot-tall, gray pyramidal tower of the George Washington Masonic Memorial, built earlier in this century with $5 million donated by three million members of the Masonic order. It's the region's tallest structure after the Washington Monument (and, like the big white needle, it's open to the public, with an elevator ride to the top). Pause en route to see things like the dioramas depicting Masonic deeds and the trowel George Washington used to lay the U.S. Capitol's cornerstone. Just south of the temple is Alexandria Union Station, much less grand than D.C.'s Union Station, but a quaint stop on Amtrak's southern route nonetheless.

Leave the Metro station and head north under the railroad tracks

Reagan
National Airport

120

Mt. Vernon Ave.

Russell Road

Commonwealth Ave.

NORTH

Braddock
Monument

Mt. Vernon Trail
to 14th St. Bridge

North
Union Street

POTOMAC RIVER

King St. Metro

Masonic
Temple   R

Park &
START

Daingerfield Road

King St.

Washington Street

Prince St.

Mt. Vernon Trail

HOW to get there   By Metro, Yellow Line to King Street Station. By car, George Washington Memorial Parkway south to Washington Street; turn right on King Street and drive 1 mile to Metro parking lot. By bike, take Mount Vernon Trail from north or south to King Street and ride 1 mile to Metro station.

DIRECTIONS for the ride

- From King Street Metro, go under tracks on King Street.
- Bear right on Russell Road.
- Follow Russell for about 30 blocks until it ends at Y intersection.
- Hard right on Mount Vernon Avenue.
- At Y intersection, bear right on Commonwealth Avenue and follow for 25 blocks.
- Pass under railroad tracks and turn left at light onto Daingerfield Road.
- First left onto Prince Street.
- Straight on Prince Street about 1 mile to North Union.
- Left on North Union.
- After 1 block, left on King Street.
- Straight for 1 mile back to King Street Metro station.

on King Street. Take the second right onto Russell Road. You are entering Rosemont, a pre–World War I suburb that the city of Alexandria annexed in 1915. Rosemont's raison d'être was the Washington, Alexandria, and Mt. Vernon electric streetcar line, which brought downtown D.C. within a nickel and eighteen minutes. (A 1909 ad promised free streetcar tickets to come view model homes priced from $750 to $1,200.) The streetcar faded away in the 1930s, but Rosemont continued to thrive and today is a well-preserved neighborhood with neat bungalows mixed in among grander houses with wraparound porches.

Russell Road whisks you through Rosemont before you start climbing the North Ridge. Located in a small traffic triangle, a cannon mounted on cobblestones and concrete marks the spot where General Edward Braddock led his troops off in 1755 to defend the western front against the French and their Indian allies. Stop at Alexandria Country Day School at the top of the hill on the left for an excellent view over the Potomac to Maryland. Also known as Shuter's

Hill, the ridge was seized by Union troops during the Civil War and laid bare so lookouts would have clear sightlines.

Rosemont segues into Del Ray, a blue-collar neighborhood built to house railroad workers for nearby Potomac Yards. (Del Ray was formerly called Potomac, but its cottages would never be confused with the plummy manses across the river in Potomac, Maryland.) The 320-acre freight yards are giving way to a massive new development called Potomac 2020. After heading downhill, double back through Rosemont along commercial Mount Vernon Avenue. Bear right onto bike-laned Commonwealth Avenue, where the trolley formerly ran on the median strip.

After again threading under the Metrorail tracks and turning left on Daingerfield Road, head east on Prince Street toward the river. The vacant traffic triangle you pass while making the turn is the former site of Hooff's Run, a creek now channeled through underground pipes.

Alexandria was intended to be a grand and great city until it was outstripped as a port, and its early architecture reflects it. Prince Street is one of Old Town's oldest and most intact thoroughfares. A series of rowhouses in the 200 block, Gentry Row, dates from 1752 to 1795; 200 Prince belonged to Robert Townshend Hooe, the city's first elected mayor. Another house belonged to Dr. James Craik, the physician at George Washington's side when he died; Craik's colleague and neighbor Dr. Elisha Cullen Dick cut the pendulum cords on the first president's clock to record the time of death. Across the street, the Greek Revival Lyceum, built as a library in 1839, has housed the city's history museum since 1985. At the corner of Prince and busy Washington Streets stands a bronze statue of R. E. Lee Camp, confederate soldier. The monument offends some, but the Virginia legislature passed a special bill in 1890 ensuring it would never be moved.

Continue down Prince (the last block is cobblestone) to North Union and visit the artsy-craftsy Torpedo Factory (which has a new waterfront "food court," à la shopping malls) before returning to the start via King Street, Old Town's busiest and boutique-iest boulevard. The corner of King and Pitt recorded the Civil War's first casualty: A

Union colonel named Ellsworth was shot dead after he tore a Confederate flag from a tavern.

Interestingly, the only marker at this corner is a tribute to James W. Jackson, the First Martyr to the Cause of Southern Independence, who was found by a coroner's inquiry to be defending his property.

Reservoir–Great Falls Run

Distance:	24-mile loop
Approximate pedaling time:	3 hours
Terrain:	Flat with two big hills
Surface:	Smooth roads, bike paths
Things to see:	Bluffs overlooking river, Glen Echo Park, Clara Barton House, Cabin John viaduct, Great Falls Tavern
Facilities:	Convenience food along route, health-food co-op, rest rooms at Glen Echo and Great Falls
Option:	Return trip through C & O Canal National Historical Park
Recommended for:	Tourists, Natural beauty

This jaunt should be dedicated to Quartermaster General Montgomery C. Meigs, a Civil War hero and engineer who designed the 10-mile-long aqueduct system that still provides Washington with fresh water. In the process he created a refreshing route for modern-day cyclists. The Meigs legacy is announced by a series of whimsical structures that now line this popular cycling route to Great Falls National Park in Maryland.

Start at the confluence of Reservoir Road and MacArthur Boulevard, near a pumping structure that Meigs disguised as a classical temple. The reservoir's grounds are populated by black vultures, ducks, and even red fox. You are in the heart of the city's Palisades enclave, dense with trees and rambling old wood-frame houses. Head west on MacArthur Boulevard, the neighborhood's main street, past such landmarks as a one-room schoolhouse and the Art Deco MacArthur Theater, now converted to a drug store. The road is wind-

C & O CANAL

MARYLAND

Great Falls Pk.
R

Cabin John Creek

Angler's
Inn

Cabin
John Viaduct

VIRGINIA

Barton House
R
Glen Echo Pk.
R

POTOMAC RIVER

MacArthur Blvd.

D.C.

Reservoir Rd.

NORTH

Park &
START

Georgetown
Reservoir

HOW to get there — From Georgetown, west on Canal Road to Arizona Avenue; turn right, and right again on MacArthur Boulevard to reach Reservoir Road intersection. From Virginia, cross Chain Bridge, right on Canal Road, left on Arizona, right on MacArthur. From Maryland, east on MacArthur to Reservoir intersection. Park in the neighborhood (note weekday restrictions on signs) or in shopping areas on MacArthur Boulevard.

DIREC-TIONS for the ride

- From MacArthur Boulevard and Reservoir Road, head west on shoulder of MacArthur. After passing Dalecarlia Reservoir, road narrows to two lanes. Cross MacArthur to off-road bike path that begins on left.

- Follow bike path to parking area for Glen Echo Park and Clara Barton National Historic Site, about 4 miles from ride start.

- Off-road path ends in another 5 miles. Follow on-road route as MacArthur Boulevard curves right past Old Angler's Inn for a long, winding climb through the woods.

- At crest of hill, turn left into Great Falls Park as Falls Road turns right. Swift descent on-road leads to visitor's center.

- Retrace steps back to Washington. Or return via C & O Canal towpath, a route that requires carrying your bike up and down several staircases on a walkway over the canal to avoid a rocky section near Great Falls. In 12 miles, at Fletcher's Boat House, cross bridge over canal. Cross Canal Road to Reservoir Road. Ride up steep hill to intersection of Reservoir and MacArthur (see Ride 14).

ing and busy, but the shoulder is wide and traffic moves slowly.

At the city line, marked by another reservoir, the boulevard narrows to a two-lane road. Switch to the bike path at left, parallel to oncoming traffic. Climb a short but steep hill to reach the Brookmont neighborhood. At the top of the hill, look to your right and you'll see the Capital Crescent Trail. You'll be riding over the Dalecarlia tunnel.

Next, the path traces a precipice high above the river. This was the old trolley route (described by John Dos Passos in his *U.S.A.* trilogy) from downtown to the country. Ruins of the old trestle remain among the sycamore trees and thorny undergrowth. For nearly seventy years the transit line's terminus was Glen Echo amusement park. After the park closed in 1968, the National Park Service acquired the land to create a cultural center. The 1921 Dentzel carousel has been restored, calliope intact, and is open spring through fall. Also preserved are the bumper-car shed and the Spanish Ballroom, still used for swing dances and concerts. This may be the world's only Art Deco ghost town—well worth a look. Reach Glen Echo by turning left onto Oxford Road, just past a small traffic circle.

Before leaving the streamlined spires of Glen Echo, visit the neighboring Clara Barton National Historic Site, a turreted Victorian house where the saintly founder of the American Red Cross spent her last fifteen years. It's open every day except national holidays.

Continuing west alongside MacArthur Boulevard, the trail meanders through the old town of Glen Echo. The historic Glen Echo Town Hall and Post Office are on your left, located on Harvard Avenue. Yes, there is also a Cornell Avenue, as well as Yale, Princeton, and Bryn Mawr. Take a short loop around the town and you'll encounter Oxford Road and Wellesley and Vassar Circles, too. Return to the bike path on MacArthur Boulevard, turn left and continue through the town of Cabin John.

Slow down to cross a bridge wide enough for only one lane of cars and one lane of bicycles. This is Meigs's great 220-foot-long aqueduct, constructed to convey 10,000 gallons of water hourly over the valley of Cabin John Creek. It still does the job and carries rush-hour traffic in style as well.

A bit up the road on the right, hearty (and organic) human food is available at the Bethesda Co-op. The next landmark, on the left, is the U.S. Navy's Carderock Division of Naval Surface Warfare Center, which resembles a mile-long Quonset hut. The shed contains a tank for testing scale models of ships. Continue parallel to MacArthur Boulevard and its clusters of Victorian houses. These hills were once alive with gold mines, opened during the Civil War and abandoned since 1935.

By now cars will be whizzing by with splinter-shaped boats mounted on their roofs. These are kayakers heading for the mouth of Mather Gorge, whose rapids test the most competitive spirits. They put in near the C & O Canal right across from Old Angler's Inn, a tavern and restaurant since 1860. It's a pricey spot to take a break, but you may need the energy for the hill leading to the entrance to Great

Falls Park. It's a long climb, so gear down and pedal easy to enjoy the smoothly-paved road through deep woods.

Stay left at the top and zoom down the other side of the same hill to arrive at the Great Falls Tavern Visitor's Center. Be sure to stop at the guard house—there's an entrance fee of $2 for cyclists and $4 for cars. The tavern was built in 1890 to serve workers on the C & O Canal. Today it is a museum. Just across the canal, footpaths and platforms present views of this ferocious section of river, where in 0.25 mile rapids drop 76 feet through a gorge. Ask a local to point out the bald-eagle nest on a river island.

Decision time: Either climb the steep hill back out of the park to double back to D.C. on the MacArthur Boulevard Trail, or return on the C & O Canal towpath, described in Ride 13.

Note: In 1996 a major flood breached the canal and ravaged its towpath. Temporary repairs were made, and the towpath is usually open. However more permanent repairs continue, and you may encounter detours. Call the Great Falls Tavern Visitor's Center at (301) 299–3613 for up-to-date information.

Upper Reaches
of Rock Creek Park

Distance:	8-mile loop
Approximate pedaling time:	1 hour
Terrain:	Very hilly
Surface:	Two-lane roads and off-road trails
Things to see:	Natural areas of Rock Creek Park
Option:	Connection to Maryland bike path
Facilities:	Rest rooms at Pierce Mill and Nature Center
Recommended for:	Natural beauty, Workout

Washington cyclists can take a midweek break in the country without leaving the city limits. This can be accomplished by touring the looping road system of northern Rock Creek Park.

This is Rock Creek's more rustic side. The park's 1,800 acres are 85 percent wooded and contain fifteen wildflower meadows comprising 400 plant species, including goldenrod, purpletop grass, thistle, and aster. A British ambassador once asked rhetorically, "What city in the world is there where a man can, within a quarter of an hour and on his own feet, get in a beautiful rocky glen such as you would find in the woods of Maine or Scotland?" Here Theodore Roosevelt would go off on rugged jaunts, and John Quincy Adams described visiting "this romantic glen, listening to the singing of a thousand birds."

Among the glades and dells of Rock Creek are great stands of tulip trees, oak, and dogwood, with an understory of alder bush, azalea, and witch hazel. The park roads have been designed to follow the undulations of these hills. Dramatic, sweeping curves provide excellent views of the gorge. Bridle paths cross the road beds at many intervals. Traffic is light except on Beach Drive, a busy commuter road on weekdays that is closed to motor traffic on weekends and holidays (see Ride 4). An off-road trail runs parallel to the portion of Beach Drive included in this ride.

Start next to the rumbling falls at historic Pierce Mill. Proceed north through the parking area with Rock Creek on your right. In 0.25 mile, turn left onto two-lane Broad Branch Road and take an immediate right on Ridge Road. Climb a steep hill for 0.5 mile. Note the rustic stone wall on the S-curve. Pass a rambling meadow retained by a split-log fence.

Bear left at a sign for the Nature Center to traverse a broad meadow with playing fields and picnic tables. Come to an intersection with a traffic light. Cross four-lane Military Road (an important Civil War supply line) to reach Oregon Avenue. (Or take the marked, off-road path that runs parallel.) This two-lane road divides a residential neighborhood from the dense woods of Rock Creek Park's western border. The rambling houses on the left are among the city's most exclusive, combining bucolic pleasures with a short commute to downtown D.C. On the right are the ruins of Fort DeRussy at the park's highest point. A hike into the woods will reveal the remains of earthworks, moats, and trenches from this Civil War site.

At Bingham Drive turn right and hang on for a steep descent down to the Rock Creek basin. You can choose between the road bed (smooth surface, no shoulders, moderate traffic) or the path at left (separate from traffic, fair surface). At Beach Drive, to avoid heavy traffic, turn right onto a much smoother off-road trail. Continue along the valley floor for about 1 mile to Joyce Road, a four-way stop. Turn right and immediately left on Ross Drive. Prepare for several steep climbs and descents through wooded highlands. Near the Nature Center, Ross Drive melts into Ridge Road. Like all good rides, this one ends with a sharp descent. Slow down for the S-curve around a picnic meadow, and return to Pierce Mill.

Option: To connect to Rock Creek Regional Park in Maryland and avoid weekday traffic on Beach Drive, keep straight on Oregon rather than turning right on Bingham Drive. Follow Oregon until it ends at Western Avenue, and turn left. Shortly thereafter turn right on Green-

Bingham Dr.

Oregon Ave.

• Fort DeRussy

Beach Dr.

Joyce Rd.

Military Rd.

Ridge Rd.

Nature Center
• R

Ross Dr.

NORTH

ROCK CREEK

Broad Branch Rd.

Connecticut Avenue

Tilden St.

Pierce Mill R
★ Park &
START

D.C.

HOW
to get
there

Heading south on Connecticut Avenue, turn left on Tilden Street to Pierce Mill. From Virginia, take Rock Creek Parkway south to Pierce Mill. Heading north on Connecticut Avenue, turn right on Tilden Street to Pierce Mill.

DIREC-TIONS for the ride

- Head north from Pierce Mill parking area.
- In 0.25 mile, left on Broad Branch Road and immediate right onto Ridge Road.
- Bear left at sign for Nature Center as Ross Road turns right.
- At Military Road traffic light, go straight. Ridge Road becomes Oregon Avenue.
- Right on Bingham Drive.
- Right on off-road trail parallel to Beach Drive. On weekends, Beach Drive is closed to vehicular traffic.
- At four-way stop, right on Joyce Road.
- First left on Ross Drive.
- Ross Drive ends at Ridge Road near Nature Center. Turn left.
- Left at bottom of long hill.
- Right into Pierce Mill parking area.

vale Street. In a few blocks, turn left on Beach Drive. Cross the bridge at Candy Cane City, a playground next to the Meadowbrook Riding Stables, to reach the Maryland bikeway through Rock Creek Regional Park, described in Ride 4. It runs about 16 miles to Lake Needwood.

Sligo–Rock Creek Weekend Loop

Distance:	13-mile loop
Approximate pedaling time:	90 minutes
Terrain:	Hilly
Surface:	Two-lane roads and off-road trails
Things to see:	Rock Creek Park, Walter Reed Annex, historic Forest Glen, Sligo Creek Park, Takoma Park
Facilities:	Restrooms at Candy Cane City. Convenience stores and rest rooms in Takoma Park
Recommended for:	Tourists, Families with children (weekends only), Natural beauty, Mostly bike paths

Think quick escape. If you live in D.C., Bethesda, Silver Spring, or Takoma Park, you can do this ride without loading the roof rack or jumping on the subway. This is my after-gardening-but-before-dinner ride. Combining aspects of Rides 4 and 21, it melds routes through two stream-valley parks with looks at two historic areas not covered elsewhere here. It's a *weekend-only* ride because it includes sections of Beach Drive that are closed to cars Saturday and Sunday but packed with commuters on weekdays.

Start at the intersection of Beach and Sherrill Drives in the D.C. portion of Rock Creek Park, about 2 miles north of the National Zoo. Head north past picnic areas, rock outcroppings, and stands of mountain laurel (the pink and white blooms come out in late May). Horse trails parallel this route, along with hiking trails maintained by the Potomac Appalachian Trail Club. Lock up your bike sometime and try one—it's easy to lose the city within the park's 1,800 acres.

Most but not all of Beach Drive is closed on weekends, but a few sections remain open so that groups can reach picnic areas by car; beware of the occasional auto. After leaving the city through a bikes-only gate, look for a playground called Candy Cane City. A marked sign on the right leads off Beach Drive and over a small bridge. Turn left into a parking lot and pass the playground and ball fields until you reach a T next to a horse pasture; this is the Meadowbrook Stable. Turn left on Meadowbrook Lane until you come to East-West Highway, a major arterial. Cross at the signal to pick up a bike path that heads north past playing fields and wetlands. Proceed to the Walter Reed Annex as described in Ride 4 (Rock Creek Park: D.C. to Maryland and Back). This time you'll pass through the architectural theme park. At the top of the winding bike path, turn left onto Linden Lane and bear right at the next fork (signed bike route).

Coast down a hill (past Ye Forest Inne, a failed resort in the 1890s and now part of Walter Reed Annex) to cross the Beltway on an overpass and cruise through the historic community of Forest Glen. Founded by the notable Carroll family in the 1700s among a 4,200-acre tract of wilderness, Forest Glen retains a country feel, with winding roads and old frame houses with broad porches. On the left St. John's Cemetery doubles as a village green. The road is tight, but the drivers courteous. At the top of the hill are railroad tracks and the former B & O railroad station.

After passing the new Forest Glen Metrorail station, cross busy Georgia Avenue at the signal and descend past Holy Cross Hospital on the right. Bear right at the bottom of the hill to pick up the Sligo Creek Hiker-Biker Trail.

Environmentally speaking, Sligo Creek has long been a poor sister to the wider, better preserved Rock Creek valley, but that may be changing. (It's hard to believe that the sometimes foul-smelling Sligo supplied water mains until 1930.) The local sewer commission plans to remove leaky pipes (think the worst) from the creek bed to a new right-of-way above the banks. Many new trees, including lovely paperbark birches, have been planted in the park, and wildflower meadows have supplanted boring expanses of lawn. Parts of the creek

HOW to get there — From the south, head north on Rock Creek Parkway and follow signs for Beach Drive/National Zoo. Stay on Beach Drive and park in picnic areas just before or after Sherrill Drive on the right. Coming crosstown, take Military Road to the Beach Drive/Ross Drive exit.

DIREC-TIONS for the ride

- From Sherrill Drive, right on Beach Drive to head north.
- From Beach Drive, turn right to enter Candy Cane City playground. Bear left and follow bike route signs out of parking lot.
- Left at T onto Meadowbrook Lane.
- Cross East-West Highway (Route 410) to pick up Rock Creek bike path north.
- Turn right past small playground to take path to Walter Reed Annex.
- Left on Linden Lane.
- Follow bike route signs across Beltway and railroad tracks.
- At top of hill, where sign reads BIKE ROUTE ENDS (ignore it), go straight to pick up Forest Glen Road through historic Forest Glen.
- Cross Georgia Avenue at signal to stay on Forest Glen Road for another 6 blocks.
- After passing Holy Cross Hospital on right, turn right onto Sligo Creek Hiker-Biker Trail.
- After crossing Piney Branch at signal, go straight onto Sligo Creek Parkway (caution—narrow road with traffic) or stay on winding bike path.
- At T, right on Maple Avenue.
- At four-way stop, left on Tulip Avenue.
- In 3 blocks at T, right on Carroll Avenue.
- At Takoma clock tower, turn right to stay on Carroll Avenue. Stay on Carroll through underpass beneath Metrorail tracks.
- Left onto Fourth Street N.W. at signal immediately after underpass.
- In 1 block, right onto Butternut Street N.W.
- At Georgia Avenue, cross at signal and turn right onto sidewalk around Walter Reed Medical Center.
- Staying on sidewalk, turn left on Fern Street to the Alaska Avenue Gate.
- Left on Alaska Avenue N.W.
- Left on Sixteenth Street (traffic).
- First right on Sherrill Drive. Return to start.

banks are being restored with native vegetation, and the number of fish species living in Sligo Creek is expected to jump from one to a dozen or so. Recently, the hiker-biker trail was extended 3.3 miles east, where it meets the trailhead of Northwest Branch (see Ride 21).

Ride on the parkway if traffic isn't too bad, or on the winding bike path if it is. There are places where the retrofitted bike path crosses very narrow brides and takes sharp turns. Let your sense of caution be your guide. At Maple Avenue, turn right to pass by Takoma Park's high-rise apartment district. This section ends at the Sam Abbott Municipal Center, named for the late rabble-rousing mayor, a socialist who fought proposed highways that would have destroyed Takoma Park. He once said, "It doesn't bother me at all that I don't have suburban decorum." Next door is a friendly city library—the only one in Maryland outside of Baltimore.

Go straight to enter the Takoma Park Historic District. Founded in 1976 in the wake of highway and other development battles, the historic district embraces parts of D.C. and two Maryland counties. The city was carved out of farms and wilderness in 1883 by developer Benjamin Franklin Gilbert; in 1904 it took off in a spurt when the Seventh-Day Adventist church moved from Battle Creek, Michigan, to make Takoma its headquarters. (SDA has moved to sober corporate headquarters in Silver Spring, leaving in its righteous wake an almost publess, dry Takoma.)

A ride up Maple Avenue reveals large, four-square homes mixed in with gingerbread Victorians dating back to the 1890s. Many have been restored. An original city boundary marker (c. 1791) sits behind an iron fence near Maple and Carroll Avenues. Turn left down Tulip Avenue to the main drag, Carroll Avenue. Here is the heart of Washington's "folk ghetto," the House of Musical Traditions, where you can buy a hammered dulcimer or take lessons in African drumming, along with other craft shops, book stores, and restaurants. A Sunday farmers' market (in season) makes a cycling destination—bring panniers.

Follow Carroll Avenue (Route 195) as it turns right toward the Takoma Metro station. Take Butternut Street N.W. in D.C. At Georgia Avenue go straight across the street and turn right onto the sidewalk

83

to ride around the Walter Reed Army Medical Center, founded in 1898. This formal campus mixes Georgian architecture with modern and features one major public attraction: the National Museum of Health and Medicine, repository of the bullet that killed Lincoln, along with other medical curios and scientific exhibits. Until the late sixties this was one of the most popular museums on the Mall; to make room for the Hirshhorn Museum, the red brick building was razed and the collection exiled to Walter Reed.

Turn left on Fern Street, staying on the sidewalk until you reach the Alaska Avenue Gate. Take a left on Alaska Avenue and another left on Sixteenth (traffic—use the sidewalk) to Sherrill Drive. Turn right and head downhill to return to the ride's starting point.

National Arboretum Loop-de-Loop

Distance:	9-mile loop
Approximate pedaling time:	1 hour
Terrain:	Rolling hills
Surface:	Smooth roads
Things to see:	Bonsai collection, azalea garden, U.S. Capitol columns, Anacostia River, ponds and streams
Facilities:	Rest rooms at Gift Shop and Japanese Gardens
Recommended for:	Tourists, Families with children, Natural beauty, Mostly bike paths

Washington has long been known as the "City of Trees." Most neighborhoods are lined by oaks, sycamores, or even ginkgo trees, and the April blooming of the Japanese cherry trees draws millions of tourists. But the most impressive year-round display can be found at the 444-acre National Arboretum in the midst of gritty Northeast Washington. Here the prevailing mood falls between virgin forest and formal garden. Many of the trees, shrubs, and herbs are so rare they attract visitors from throughout the world.

Founded in 1927 under the auspices of the U.S. Department of Agriculture, the arboretum blooms from March through October. In winter the colors become considerably more muted, but the collection of dwarf conifers, the frozen ponds, and the tall wheat-colored grasses make off-season visits worthwhile. Summer visitors are rewarded by the sight of vast lily pads with their pink and white blooms. Ostensibly a research facility for botanists, the arboretum is one of the more graceful and serene parks in Washington.

This suggested tour loops around the grounds three times to

NORTH

ANACOSTIA RIVER

Conifer Rd.

Holly Spring Rd.

Hickey Hill Rd.

Meadow Rd.

Valley Rd.

Crabtree Rd.

Hickey La.

Springhouse Rd.

Beechwood Rd.

Ellipse Rd.

Capitol Columns

New York Avenue

Park & START

Gift Shop

Eagle Nest Rd.

Azalea Rd.

R St. N.E.

Azalea Rd.

Bladensburg Rd.

M St. N.E.

HOW to get there   From Capitol Hill, take Maryland Avenue to M Street entrance. From downtown, take New York Avenue to service road on right after Bladensburg Road. From Maryland, take Route 50 West to New York Avenue and follow signs to service road. Park at information center and gift shop.

**DIREC-
TIONS**
for the ride

- By bike, head west on Azalea Road past gift shop.
- At Rhododendron Valley Road, bear left to stay on Azalea Road.
- Azalea Road becomes Crabtree Road.
- At pond, bear right on Hickey Hill Road.
- At Y intersection, bear right on Conifer Road.
- At Y intersection, bear left and then right on Hickey Lane. Return to start.
- Head west on Azalea Road.
- At pond, bear left on Valley Road.
- Right on Meadow Road.
- Bear left at Y intersection.
- Left on Conifer Road and return to start.
- West on Azalea Road.
- Left on Ellipse Road to see U.S. Capitol columns.
- Right on Beechwood Road.
- Right on Meadow Road.
- Left on Holly Spring Road.
- Left on Conifer Road and return to start.

cover most of its 9 miles of lightly traveled roads. Many are unmarked, so you may find it difficult to follow this route exactly. All the roads are bikeable, though. If you miss a turn, just follow the signs back to the gift shop. You can pick up a *Visitor's Guide,* which includes an excellent map.

The ride starts near the National Bonsai Collection. Housed in a Japanese-style pavilion, the bonsai trees are up to 350 years old but only a few feet high. Their disposition results from generations of careful "training" by Japanese horticulturists, who donated their life's work in honor of our bicentennial. These tiny ginkgoes, maples, spruces, and crab apples form an alluring landscape in miniature.

Starting just past the gift shop at the entrance, the ride begins with a steep climb up to a precipice with a view of the mausoleums of

historic Mt. Olivet Cemetery across Bladensburg Road. In spring the 65,000 azaleas on this hillock burst out in pink, purple, orange, and scarlet blooms. There's also a stand of a type of dawn redwood that exists nowhere else outside of China. Cruising downhill at high speed, pass flowering crab apples and a bird garden. The road continues to descend into a dark valley of ferns. Cross a stream bed and bear right at a pond (often full of geese) to climb again for a view of the Anacostia River. This slow-moving tidal branch of the Potomac is here seen at its bucolic best.

Heading north, the cyclist encounters Japanese, Korean, and Chinese gardens complemented by pagodas, bridges, and other structures of the East. A cruise past neat rows of Japanese maples completes the first leg. Starting again from the parking area, repeat the first section of the ride until reaching Beech Spring Pond, where you turn left instead of bearing right. Near a second pond, by a fragrant area of lilacs and hibiscus, turn right to cross a broad meadow. Take the next two left turns to traverse what looks like pristine farmland on the way back to the start.

The final leg affords a look at a hillside planted with 1,500 dwarf conifers such as yew, cedar, and pine. Like the bonsai, the dwarf conifers have been sculpted into shapely miniatures. Unlike the potted Japanese trees, they are planted in the ground, giving the impression of a troll forest. Another quirky feature on the grounds is the collection of the original Corinthian columns from the east portico of the U.S. Capitol. The columns were dismantled in the 1950s when the east front was remodeled. They were re-erected here in 1990 in their original configuration—freestanding columns eerily girding nothing. The latest addition to the arboretum is a collection of bonsai trained in North America. Two projects are on the boards: a National Bird Garden and a National Grove of State Trees.

Except in spring, when the azaleas burst, the arboretum is never as crowded as other Washington attractions. The roads all run oneway. Since most people walk the grounds, you won't encounter many automobiles. The only drawback is that the arboretum is not easily reached by bike paths, on-road routes, or Metrorail.

C & O Canal
Georgetown to Great Falls

Distance:	15 miles, one-way
Approximate pedaling time:	3 hours
Terrain:	Flat
Surface:	Packed dirt with some rocks
Things to see:	Working locks of nineteenth-century canal, rapids and dams of Potomac River, lockkeepers' houses and other historic structures
Facilities:	Rest room, snacks, bike and canoe rentals, fishing gear at Fletcher's Boat House and Swain's Lock; snacks and boat rides at Great Falls
Options:	Extend ride to Seneca, Maryland; return via MacArthur Boulevard; join Ride 26; join Ride 25
Recommended for:	Tourists, Families with children, Natural beauty, Mostly bike paths, Countryside

The Chesapeake & Ohio Canal was destined to be a financial flop even before the first spadeful of earth was turned in 1828. The reason: the rise of railroads. By 1850, when canal construction stretched 184 miles from Georgetown in Washington to Cumberland, Maryland, in the Appalachian Mountains, freight trains had siphoned away much of the canal's business.

In 1924 the obsolete canal closed for good. In the 1950s even the *Washington Post* advocated filling in the remains to create a new commuter road. In stepped U.S. Supreme Court Justice William O. Dou-

SENECA

Observation Deck
Great Falls Tavern ℞

C & O CANAL

NORTH

495

Beltway

POTOMAC RIVER

• Stairs to MacArthur Blvd.

• Glen Echo Park
  ℞

BROOKMONT
MD

Capital Crescent Trail

Fletcher's Boat House •
  ℞

GEORGETOWN
RESERVOIR

C & O Canal
Trail

Park &
START

ROOSEVELT
ISLAND

Thompsons Boat Center ℞

HOW
to get
there
From north, Rock Creek Parkway to Thompson's parking lot; turn right. From the Mall, Virginia Avenue west across Rock Creek Parkway to Thompson's parking lot. From Virginia, Theodore Roosevelt or Memorial Bridge to Rock Creek Parkway to Thompson's parking lot. By Metro, Blue or Orange Line to Foggy Bottom/GWU, about 1-mile walk via New Hampshire and Virginia avenues.

DIREC-TIONS for the ride

- Exit Thompson Boat Center toward Rock Creek Parkway.
- Turn left immediately on Rock Creek bike path.
- After crossing concrete bridge, turn left on brick trail. This is trailhead for towpath of C & O Canal.
- After crossing Twenty-eighth and Twenty-ninth Streets in Georgetown, trail becomes packed dirt.
- At Thirty-fourth Street, cross footbridge to other side of canal. Trail continues on Potomac River side.
- Follow milestones to Great Falls. Note: Cyclists must dismount and walk near Great Falls for about a quarter mile.

Options: You may return via the route described in Ride 10 by taking the park road up the hill out of Great Falls. At top of hill, turn right onto MacArthur Boulevard. Right on Chain Bridge Road to pick up C & O Canal for return to Thompson's.

You may join Ride 26 by continuing on the towpath to White's Ferry, Maryland.

You may join Ride 25 by continuing past Great Falls to Pennyfield Lock Road. Turn right on Pennyfield, climb a hill, and turn left on River Road.

glas, an avid birder and hiker who led a cavalcade of decision-makers on a nature walk that changed many minds. In 1977 President Jimmy Carter dedicated the C & O Canal National Historical Park in honor of Douglas.

The route follows the unpaved towpath, designed for mules to pull oblong barges carrying coal down the canal. Though bumpy in places (skinny tires, beware), the path offers many rewards for cyclists, joggers, and birders. Today mules still pull replicas of the old canal barges for pleasure rides down the canal. Injecting a linear slice of nature right into the city, the canal is lined by a canopy of sycamore, red maple, sassafras, and willow trees, along with mushrooms, wild raspberries, and wildflowers such as blue phlox, Queen Anne's lace, and mayapples. The bird density is three times that of the regional average. While pedaling my mountain bike at 15 miles per hour, I've spotted barred owls, pileated woodpeckers, red-tailed hawks, and bluebirds. Spouts that bypass the locks create little falls rumbling over boulders. Turnarounds for barges have degraded into freshwater swamps full of cattails and hawk roosts. The still, opaque waters of the canal itself are alive with carp and turtles.

Canal cruisers will begin their rides at the Harry T. Thompson Boat Center, the starting point for many rides described in this book. Turn left out of the parking lot and left again onto a brick path marked as the beginning of the C & O park. Passing through Georgetown, you'll encounter the first canal lock. This begins a ride to Great Falls headed ever-so-slightly uphill—a total of 190 feet in 15 miles. The entire route is restored with working locks and charming fieldstone lockkeepers' houses. Brown mile-markers along the way make it easy to find canal highlights and ruins.

For example:

• Mile 0: The towpath passes under the grand arches of Key Bridge. Francis Scott Key actually lived near here in a mansion dismantled in the 1940s. A footpath leads up to M Street and the many shops and historic houses of the old port of Georgetown.

• Mile 0.1: Next to a vast green boathouse in Georgetown, find the remains of the Old Alexandria Aqueduct, which spanned the Potomac. This is also the starting point for the Capital Crescent Trail, which follows an old railroad right-of-way to downtown Bethesda. See Ride 5 for a complete loop incorporating this rail-to-trail stretch.

• Mile 1.8: Look across the Potomac for a view of a wet-weather waterfall on the Virginia side.

• Mile 2.4: Another boathouse with a country flavor, Fletcher's, rents mountain bikes, boats, and fishing gear.

• Mile 2.7: Pass under the old B & O railroad bridge, which now carries the Capital Crescent Trail away from the river, across the canal.

• Mile 4.2: Bike ramp to Chain Bridge and Ride 16.

• Mile 4.7: The "feeder" draws water from the river to discharge into the canal at lock 5. Look closely at the curved red sandstone of the locks to find initials and symbols carved in by the stone cutters.

- Mile 6.6: A 0.5-mile walking path connects the towpath to Glen Echo Park, described in Ride 10.
- Mile 7.3: Pass under the 220-foot-long arch of the Cabin John Bridge, an engineering marvel of the 1850s.
- Mile 12.6: Enter Widewater, a broad section of the canal that looks like a mountain lake. The going gets a bit rough for a quarter mile where you may have to walk your bike over rocks and boulders. To avoid this, you can cross over the canal at mile 13.5 and ride on the opposite side for a while. To get back, you'll have to carry your bike up and down several stairs on a walkway over the canal. I'd chose the stairs over the rocks, but either way you'll have to carry your bike a short distance.
- Mile 15: Arrive at Great Falls Tavern, a hostelry built in 1831 and restored in 1942. Today the whitewashed structure houses a museum. Be sure to view the spectacular falls from the platform. From this location, looking 20 degrees to the right, you can spot an active bald-eagle nest spreading out among the high branches of a sycamore. It's on the banks of a river island.

Option: The length of this ride will satisfy most cyclists, but if you want to explore the canal further, you can ride another 7 miles to Seneca Creek. The creek is close to several old quarries from which the stone for the Smithsonian castle was pulled. Points of interest en route include Swain's Lock, the site of an old lockkeeper's house now used to rent canoes and bikes (301–299–9006) and sell snacks. After Pennyfield lock, site of the ruins of historic Tobytown, the river grows quite wide. Just up to the left, a bottomland marsh has been designated a waterfowl sanctuary. It's full of wildflowers, fish, and herons as well as ducks and geese.

The quality of the towpath surface degenerates after Seneca Creek. Although riding the entire 184-mile route (with detours and overnight stops) is a popular "once-in-a-lifetime" experience, the Georgetown-Seneca route offers years' worth of exploration. I've yet to exhaust my interest. If you would like to learn more about the canal, you might want to join a free bicycle tour led by a National Park Service ranger. Every Saturday during summer months, a group starts at 9:00 A.M.

from the Canal visitor's center on Thomas Jefferson Street in Georgetown. The ride goes to Great Falls and takes about 3 hours. Bikers are on their own after that to explore as they wish and ride back. No reservations are required, but you might call to be sure the trip has not been canceled due to weather (202–653–5190).

Note: In January 1996 a major flood breached the canal and ravaged its towpath. Repairs were made, and the trail is now open. However, more permanent fixes are continuing; sections of the towpath may be under repair. Call the Great Falls Tavern Visitor's Center at (301) 299–3613 for up-to-date information.

Tour of South Arlington

Distance:	17-mile loop
Approximate pedaling time:	2 hours
Terrain:	Rolling
Surface:	Excellent off-road trail with center stripe, boardwalk, ramps, and bridges
Things to see:	"Contemporary urban development," wildflower meadow, bird sanctuary, pretty neighborhoods, creek, and Potomac shores
Facilities:	Rest rooms, parks, and water fountains en route
Recommended for:	Tourists, Families with children, Mostly bike paths

At 25.7 square miles, Arlington is the smallest county in the United States, but it has resolved to become one of the best municipalities for cycling, with more than 75 miles of trails and on-street routes. Arlington's reputation as a cycling mecca was solidified in 1989 with the Virginia debut of the Tour duPont, America's biggest pro cycling race. Former Tour de France winner Greg Lemond and other world-class riders contested a stage of this two-week race along the George Washington Parkway.

Though the area that is now Arlington was discovered by Captain John Smith in 1607 and first mapped out as part of the District of Columbia in 1791, it remained unsettled for much longer. Small farms arrived only around 1850, and government workers in search of suburbs to settle came around 1910. Farms and log cabins could be found within its boundaries into this century. Well before all that,

Custis Bike Trail

Metro/Rosslyn

66

Sycamore St.

Metro/East
Falls Church

50

T. ROOSEVELT
ISLAND ᴿ

Park & ᴿ
★ START

Arlington
National
Cemetery

Arlington Blvd.

POTOMAC RIVER

W & OD Trail ᴿ

Four-Mile Run Trail

395

Shirley Highway

Mount Vernon Trail

Anderson
Bike Path

SHIRLINGTON
VILLAGE
ᴿ

ᴿ

NORTH

HOW
to get
there

From Washington, cross the Roosevelt Bridge and
turn north onto the George Washington Parkway. In
0.5 mile, turn into Roosevelt Island parking lot. Fron
Alexandria, north on George Washington Parkway. By
Metro, take Blue or Orange Line to Rosslyn; ride toward Key
Bridge and pick up bike route before crossing.

- From parking lot, north on bike path and up biker/hiker bridge over George Washington Parkway.
- Stay on bike path; cross Fort Meyer Drive at Key Bridge. Follow bike path on sidewalk next to Lee Highway. Custis Bike Trail begins here, behind a concrete sound barrier.
- West for 5 miles on trail.
- Right at T intersection remaining on Custis bike path. In less than a tenth of a mile, left at second T intersection onto W & OD bike bath heading east. (To head to East Falls Church Metrorail station, turn right on W & OD Trail and head 1 mile to East Falls Church Park, then right on North Roosevelt.)
- On W & OD Trail, head southwest under Arlington and Wilson Boulevards and Walter Reed Drive.
- At Columbia Pike, W & OD and Four Mile Run bike paths split. Bear right onto Four-Mile Run path under Columbia Pike.
- Near Interstate 395, right on South Randolph Street and left on South 28th Street. Follow bike path signs onto sidewalk on north side of street, then around corner to pedestrian overpass over Shirley Highway (395).
- Left on Custis Road.
- Left on West Glebe Road. Use sidewalk to reach South Glebe Road, which leads to Wayne F. Anderson Bikeway (busy and poorly marked).
- Follow sidewalk over Route 1 to passage under railroad tracks leading to Mount Vernon Trail.
- Left on Mount Vernon Trail. Follow signs to Rosslyn and take path under Memorial Bridge (rather than bearing left, which will divert you across the George Washington Parkway toward Arlington Cemetery—see Ride 1). Right into parking lot.

the original inhabitants were probably the Doegs and Necostins of the Algonquin tribes. Today's Arlington is a rapidly developing area with about 140,000 residents. Charming and historic bungalow neighborhoods stand cheek-by-jowl with new high-rises and highways.

This trip, which uses sections for four bike paths, begins at Theodore Roosevelt Island, a park of natural beauty, all too close to Rosslyn, the high-rise district (and home of *USA Today*). A trip down the interstate will take you into the heart of the county.

Along with parts of Route 70 in Colorado, this section of Interstate 66 through Arlington is one of the few interstate highways in the United States that not only allows but encourages cycling. Like its Rocky Mountain counterpart, Interstate 66 features a well-thought-out multiuse trail made possible by spectacular engineering. The path soars well above the road bed on buff-colored concrete barriers that also muffle road noise from the adjoining neighborhoods and crisscrosses the four-lane road on high ramps and bridges. The grades are surprisingly steep and frequent. It's a trip through a manufactured mountain range that I call the Concrete Cotswolds.

That said, the route (also known officially as the Custis Memorial Trail) is darned handy. Its many direct connections include Key Bridge into Georgetown, the Theodore Roosevelt Island Pedestrian/ Bicycle Bridge leading to the Mount Vernon Trail, the W & OD Trail, and the Four-Mile Run Trail. It's also the middle link for an uninterrupted 64-mile off-road ride through northern Virginia (which can be extended by crossing into Washington or Maryland).

Moreover, the Interstate 66 trail is practical. Connections to at least a dozen neighborhoods and commercial areas allow residents to commute or shop without a car. The signs on the trail point you exactly where you're going; for a change, they're at least as good as the road signs.

All this came about as a result of a twenty-five-year battle to build Interstate 66, originally conceived as an eight-lane superhighway. Neighborhood groups sued to save their homes and trees, while the highway engineers compromised by cutting back on auto lanes, adding a median for Metrorail, planning parks and sound barriers, and designing this impressive bike byway. Opposition never dissolved entirely, but the road did get built.

About the only thing lacking along Interstate 66 is scenery. Mostly you see banal high-rises, zooming autos, and plastic-looking plantings. It does, however, get you to where you're going: the much more bucolic Four-Mile Run Trail, which meets at a wildflower meadow at Interstate 66 near the Beltway and the East Falls Church Metrorail station.

Four-Mile Run forms the second side of a triangular route around Arlington. The creek serves as the natural border between Arlington County and Alexandria City. Close by its southern section you can find an original D.C. boundary marker, an old quarry, a meadow preserve, and the remains of an old bungalow-and-cottage neighborhood that was divided by highway construction. The path is broad and smooth and is bisected by a dotted yellow line, which should be standard equipment on all trails. Head along the creek's south bank into Bon Air Park, where there is a rose garden well worth seeing in season.

Continue through a valley into Glen Carlyn Park, which blooms with mountain laurel, dogwood, and azalea in spring. A waterfall marks the location of an old mill. Excursion steam trains once stopped here to pick up water for their locomotives. This is Arlington's own fall line, signifying the end of the coastal plain and the commencement of the Piedmont Plateau. George Washington once surveyed the site. Look for a historical marker. More history: Near South Fourth Street, just off the trail, is the 1742 Ball-Sellers House, once owned by George Washington's tailor. The W & OD bike path and Four-Mile Run Trail merge periodically or run parallel at this point.

After crossing under Arlington Boulevard, the route bifurcates into low and high roads. The high road offers vistas, but the low road (actually part of the W & OD Trail) is much safer. At Columbia Pike, the W & OD trail takes the high road over the street; follow the Four-Mile Run bike path under this busy street. After passing through a broad forest, you exit not into a meadow but into a very urban area, replete with a fording of Interstate 395.

Adjacent to 395 is Shirlington Village, a former strip shopping mall that has been reconstituted as a "neotraditional" development that's supposed to recall an old-fashioned brick-lined Main Street. It's a place to stroll or have an ice-cream cone, and there's a bike shop on the main drag. Pick up the trail again to cross Interstate 395, through neighborhood streets to the Anderson bike path. This parallels Four-Mile Run to where it drains into the Potomac, near a rail yard and Reagan National Airport. At this transportation nexus, turn left onto the Mount Vernon Trail, which takes you safely back to Roosevelt Island.

Tour of North Arlington

Distance:	10 miles
Approximate pedaling time:	1 hour
Terrain:	Rolling
Surface:	Well-maintained suburban roads and off-road bike paths
Things to see:	Gulf Branch Nature Center and Potomac Overlook Regional Park
Facilities:	Rest rooms at Potomac Overlook Regional Park
Option:	Connection to C & O Canal towpath (Ride 14) and Capital Crescent Loop (Ride 5) via Chain Bridge; via major hill
Recommended for:	Tourists, Natural beauty

You live in North Arlington and are looking for a short, fun ride you can fit into a busy schedule. Or you'd like to know an easy way across Chain Bridge so you can follow the C & O towpath into Georgetown for brunch, out to Great Falls for a picnic, or even to Bethesda via the Capital Crescent Trail. Or maybe you live on the Maryland side of the Potomac and would like to explore a little bit of Arlington.

Here's a convenient ride that loops around Arlington's suburban highlands, perched high above the Potomac River in the county's northern corner. It connects a few very rideable artery roads with a stream-side bike path to form a simple 10-mile loop.

Start at Potomac Overlook Regional Park, which features tennis courts, playing fields, a nature center, and a picnic area.

Exit the park via Marcy Road and turn right onto Military Road.

HOW to get there

From Washington or Maryland, cross the Potomac River at Chain Bridge. If driving, bear left onto Route 120, North Glebe Road. Take first exit at top of hill, turn left onto overpass, then left again onto Military Road. Turn left on Marcy Road to parking at Potomac Overlook Regional Park. If bicycling from Chain Bridge, ride straight uphill on Forty-first Street after crossing river. Continue at dead-end onto steep bike path, then turn left on North Randolph Street to access Route 120 overpass and Military Road.

DIREC-TIONS for the ride

- Exit Potomac Overlook Regional Park on Marcy Road.
- Right onto Military Road.
- At bottom of long hill, where Military narrows to two lanes, dismount and walk your bike across Military. Here, at Taylor Park, follow a narrow bike path into the woods.
- Continue on bike path as it crosses North Vernon and Vermont Streets.
- Left onto North 28th Street, directly across from Marymount College, at the bike path's end.
- Immediate right onto Yorktown Boulevard, which passes beneath North Glebe Road.
- Right on George Mason Drive. At dead end, continue straight onto short bike path leading to separate section of George Mason.
- Right on Williamsburg Boulevard.
- Left on North Glebe Road (Route 120) at traffic light.
- Right on Old Glebe Road at white church.
- Right on Military Road. (Or, to access Chain Bridge, continue straight onto the overpass and follow the directions under "Option" below.)
- Left on Marcy Road to start/finish at Potomac Overlook Regional Park.

Option: To connect this ride with the C & O Canal towpath or Capital Crescent Trail via Chain Bridge, follow Old Glebe Road straight onto the overpass over North Glebe instead of turning right on Military Road. Bear right on the other side, then turn left onto North Randolph Street. Look for a bike path entrance on the right—it's next to a log-cabin-style house—and follow it down a steep stretch to North 41st Street and a small parking area. Follow the marked bike lane through a busy intersection and directly onto the protected sidewalk across the bridge. On the Maryland side of the bridge, there's a hiker–biker ramp providing direct access to the canal towpath. Turn left to head in the direction of Great Falls, or right to reach Georgetown or the Capital Crescent Trail.

At the bottom of the hill, where the road narrows to two lanes, turn left to cross Military Road (carefully!) and follow the bike path that leads off into the woods. The path alternates between hard-packed dirt and pavement as it winds its way up this narrow, wooded watershed.

Emerge from the trees, and return to regular roads, across from Marymount College. Turn left onto North 28th Street, and then immediately right onto Yorktown Boulevard. Following a few up-and-down blocks through this well-kept neighborhood, turn right onto George Mason Drive. Cars would face a dead end here, but you can continue straight onto the short section of bike path that crosses a stream and connects to another stretch of George Mason Drive. Ride on for a few more blocks, then turn right onto Williamsburg Boulevard.

Williamsburg, following a short steep hill, ends at a stop light. Turn left here onto North Glebe Road, Route 120, which leads to Chain Bridge. Rather than follow this road all the way to the river, turn right onto Old Glebe Road at the big white church. This original route to the river passes by some nice, older cottages before connecting with Military Road.

On your right is the new Ethan Allen Park, the former site of one of many defensive positions ringing Washington during the Civil War. Built by troops from Vermont, the fort was named after Vermont's famous Revolutionary War commander. An exhibit provides a visual display of the ring of forts and which saw action.

Turn right onto Military to return to Marcy Road. On the way, stop and explore Gulf Branch Nature Center. You can park your bikes here and follow a narrow ravine trail down to the shore of the Potomac. This is a favorite spot for fishing or for just viewing the river up close.

For views from a higher vantage point, explore Potomac Overlook Park's network of short trails. But not by bike—Arlington is cyclist-friendly, as this ride will have shown, but these trails are for hikers only.

Neighborhoods of Northwest D.C.

Distance:	13-mile loop
Approximate pedaling time:	2 hours
Terrain:	Hilly
Surface:	City roads, potholes and all
Things to see:	Historic Logan Circle, row-house neighborhoods, Fort Stevens, Takoma Park, Gold Coast, lower Rock Creek Park, Dupont Circle
Facilities:	Along the route
Option:	Trip to downtown Takoma Park farmers' market
Recommended for:	Tourists (with caution)

Here's a ride that takes you through a part of Washington that tourists rarely see—the places beyond the monuments where people actually live. The route meanders through row-house neighborhoods both historic and of more recent vintage. Catch a bit of Takoma Park's New Age funk before visiting the site where the South almost won the Civil War, then see one of the capital's premier upper-middle-class neighborhoods before swinging through Rock Creek Park to urbane Dupont Circle.

Let me add a caveat: This route is for a special breed of rider—the city biker. These intrepid pedalers don't mind dressing from head to toe in canary yellow, painting their helmets blaze orange, installing expensive puncture-proof tubes, or occasionally sharing an 8-foot-wide street with an 8-foot-wide bus. They seem to enjoy themselves even while carrying locks as heavy as their bike frames and stopping for lights every 2 blocks. The rewards are seeing the urban fabric at a range close enough to explore crooked streets, read historical markers, and discover neighborhood haunts.

Some people will never know these pleasures. Cowed by traffic and poor road maintenance, they stick to bike paths and country lanes. Basically, they're exhibiting good common sense, but I still think they're missing out. Try this ride on a Sunday morning, when traffic is at a minimum. Remember to bring along extra tubes, coins for pay phones, and, ideally, a buddy for this and other urban rides described in this book.

Start at historic Logan Circle, named for the Civil War general John A. Logan. The Civil War was the neighborhood's heyday. Gilded Age Washingtonians built preposterously large Victorian houses featuring turrets, finials, widow's walks, and any other architectural doodads they could think of. The remarkable thing is that the Circle and its surrounding blocks have remained intact, even thrived with renovation in recent years. The Circle itself was recently restored when two extra traffic lanes were removed in favor of grass and shrubs.

Head north up a steep hill that is Thirteenth Street. You're in the midst of another architecturally interesting, but fairly gritty, neighborhood (Columbia Heights), so be careful. At the heights pass the magnificent edifice of Cardozo High, home to a famous marching band, and keep your eyes peeled for a bike-route sign pointing to Takoma Park via Third Street.

The scene remains urban but loses some of its grit in favor of green, for the houses of the Brightwood area are carefully tended and are surrounded by small lawns, azaleas, and evergreens. A former farming community that was developed with row houses in the early twentieth century, it's the type of place where people set up a transistor radio on the front porch to listen to a ball game while cutting the grass with an old push mower.

The ride heads due north across short hills on straight, quiet streets. Near the apex of the city of Washington, take a short detour to the area's first real suburb, Takoma Park, Maryland. Built after 1883 to provide inexpensive housing connected to the city by rail and streetcar, Takoma Park today is an amalgamation of many things: grand Queen Anne houses and tiny bungalows; tie-dyed types who

NORTH

Carroll Ave.
main drag of Takoma Pk
Cedar St.
5th St.
MARYLAND

Piney Branch
Tuckerman St.
16th St.
Quakenbos
Ft. Stevens
D.C.

Carter Barron
Colorado Ave.
8th St.
BRIGHTWOOD

Blagden Ave.
Gold Coast
Sherman Circle

Pierce Mill
Kansas Ave.

Rock Creek Bike Path

13th St.
Cardozo High
COLUMBIA HEIGHTS

Dupont Circle

P Street exit
P St.
Logan Circle
★ START

HOW to get there   From Dupont Circle Metro, take Dupont Circle exit and cross the circle to P Street heading east. Ride 6 blocks to Logan Circle. From downtown, take Thirteenth Street north from Pennsylvania Avenue. From Capitol Hill, take Massachusetts Avenue west to Thirteenth Street and turn right.

**DIREC-
TIONS
for the ride**

- Start at Logan Circle at the intersection of Vermont and Rhode Island Avenues and Thirteenth Street N.W.
- Head north about 25 blocks (2.5 miles) on Thirteenth Street.
- Watch for sign pointing to bike route to Takoma Park. Soft right on Kansas Avenue.
- Left at Eighth Street to enter Brightwood neighborhood.
- In about 20 blocks, right on Tuckerman Street.
- In 4 blocks, left on Fifth Street N.W.
- Ride 5 blocks to Cedar Street N.W. To visit Takoma Park, Maryland, turn right on Cedar, which turns into Carroll Avenue (main street) after crossing under railroad tracks. To return to downtown D.C., turn left on Cedar and left on Piney Branch Road.
- Visit Fort Stevens (on left near Quackenbos Street).
- Continue on Piney Branch (becomes Thirteenth Street) to Colorado Avenue (signed bike route). Turn right.
- At Fourteenth Street, quick left and right to remain on Colorado Avenue.
- Left at Seventeenth Street.
- In 2 short blocks, right on Blagden Avenue.
- Take Blagden Avenue to Beach Drive in Rock Creek Park.
- Turn right on Beach Drive, then immediate left on Broad Branch.
- Left through small parking lot to Pierce Mill.
- At Pierce Mill, join Rock Creek bike path heading south.
- In about 3 miles, take parkway exit marked for Dupont Circle.
- At top of exit ramp, right on P Street.
- Left on Twentieth Street to reach Dupont Circle Metro station (bike racks available) or continue around Dupont Circle and eastward on P Street to return to Logan Circle.

never stopped being hippies and young lawyers; and quiet suburban living and city amenities. A good reason to stop here is the food. On Sundays a farmers' market fills part of Carroll Avenue, and there are good cafes and bakeries nearby as well. For now, at least, Takoma Park is also a suburb without malls. In 1995, development plans that would change that distinction began to make headway with the local government. Brick-lined Carroll Avenue is a real Main Street, complete with a clocktower and a pharmacy run by a gentleman everyone calls "Doc."

On the way back into town, stop at reconstructed Fort Stevens to peer over the same battlements where President Lincoln nervously watched the troops of Confederate General Jubal Early advance on the underdefended capital in 1864. Bullets whizzed by Abe's stovepipe hat until Lt. Colonel Oliver Wendell Holmes supposedly barked, "Get down, you fool!" Early was soon repelled, however. Today the site is mostly grass, with only a few cannons, but a little imagination reconstructs the scene.

Though heading south toward the city center, you will soon leave urbanized areas behind. Colorado and Blagden Avenues cut diagonally across the street grid through the Gold Coast, a wealthy neighborhood with large Tudor houses. You will be coasting here, as the grades are all downhill. Soon you will arrive via Carter Barron Amphitheatre at Pierce Mill in Rock Creek Park. Take the Rock Creek Park bike path south and exit at Dupont Circle, the most cosmopolitan neighborhood in Washington. There are dozens of embassies, historic houses, movie theaters, art galleries, and bookshops in this historic district. After exploring the area on foot, you can either ride the 6 blocks east back to Logan Circle or jump on Metrorail's Red Line.

Dupont–Georgetown–Cleveland Park Loop

Distance:	7-mile loop
Approximate pedaling time:	2 hours
Terrain:	Hilly
Surface:	City roads
Things to see:	Phillips Gallery, Washington Cathedral, four historic districts, Embassy Row
Facilities:	All along the route
Recommended for:	Tourists

If you could only block out the traffic, this would be the city ride that would make you forget you're in the city, for these are both Washington's leafiest and most affluent neighborhoods, each with its own character. Georgetown, which existed as a thriving port long before the District of Columbia was conceived, has its brick sidewalks, cobblestone streets, and absurdly narrow row houses; Dupont Circle, its bistro and bookstore nightlife; Cleveland Park, its rambling wooden houses and big shade trees; and Embassy Row, its mansions that could have been plucked from Gatsby's North Shore. A stop along the way, the National Cathedral, features rolling grounds punctuated by flowering trees, and an herb garden that would be the envy of its English progenitors.

To avoid some of the heavy traffic, this ride would be best early Saturday morning. Keep in mind that parking is very sparse and limited to two hours. The ride should be taken at a very slow pace to enjoy views of gardens and stop to read plaques. Start at the Q Street entrance to the Dupont Circle Metro. The neighborhood's nerve center across the street is Kramer Books & Afterwords Cafe, which serves up spinach quiche with its Spinoza. After fortifying body and mind, head

NORTH

Cleveland Park

Wisconsin Ave.

Massachusetts Ave.

36th St.

Ordway St.

Woodley Rd.

M Metro

34th St.

Connecticut Ave.

National Cathedral

U.S. Naval Observatory

Wisconsin Ave.

Mass. Ave.

Whitehaven St.

35th St.

Sheridan Circle

Dupont Circle Metro
Park &
START

Q St.

23rd St.

P St.

GEORGETOWN

HOW to get there — By Metrorail, Red Line to Dupont Circle station, Q Street exit. From Maryland via Rock Creek Parkway, take P Street exit, P Street east to Twentieth Street, turn left to reach Q Street Metro. From Maryland via Connecticut Avenue, south to Q Street.

DIREC-TIONS for the ride

- From Q Street entrance to Dupont Circle Metro, head south on Twentieth Street 2 blocks to P Street. Turn right.
- In 3 blocks, right on Twenty-third Street and immediately left on Q Street.
- Cross Wisconsin Avenue in Georgetown; jog right and then left on Q Street again.
- Right on Thirty-fifth Street.
- Right on Whitehaven Street.
- Left on Wisconsin Avenue (heavy traffic for 10 blocks).
- Right through arched entrance to National Cathedral grounds.
- Exit Cathedral grounds and turn right on Woodley Road.
- Left on Thirty-sixth Street in Cleveland Park.
- In 5 blocks, right on Ordway Street.
- In 2 blocks, right on Thirty-fourth Street (heavy traffic).
- In about 7 blocks, left on Massachusetts Avenue (bike route on sidewalk).
- Stay on sidewalk to Sheridan Circle at Twenty-third Street.
- Go around circle to stay on Massachusetts. In 2 blocks, left on Q Street.
- Return to Dupont Circle Metro.

for P Street, a lively corridor of restaurants, boutiques, and coffeehouses. It's hard to believe that before 1873 this urbane row was a humble creek surrounded by farmland. Within thirty years this was the most fashionable address in Washington, by 1950 a slum, and now again pricey and restored.

Cross the 1914 Buffalo Bridge to Q Street for an introduction to some of Georgetown's finer houses. Farther up Q Street is Dumbarton Oaks, a palatial estate owned by Harvard University and open to the public for limited hours. Its attractions include a fantastic formal garden and a museum (designed by Philip Johnson) of pre-Columbian art. Cross Wisconsin Avenue, one of Washington's busiest shopping streets, and ride through more blocks of ornate old houses until Q Street ends.

After pedaling uphill and fighting Wisconsin Avenue traffic, you arrive some 400 feet above the level of the Potomac. The climb will be rewarded by a visit to one of the world's largest churches, the Washington Cathedral (National Cathedral). From some angles on the Potomac's south bank, the limestone towers of this Gothic wonder actually loom over the Capitol dome. The cathedral was undertaken in 1907 using medieval construction methods and wasn't completed until 1990. There are some modern details, such as stained-glass windows commemorating the moon landing, and a gargoyle that parodies a modern lawyer on the run. There's an observation deck in one of three towers, a gift shop, a brass-rubbing center, and a small commercial greenhouse.

The cathedral borders Cleveland Park, Washington's newest historic district and unofficial Volvo capital of the free world. Its residents tend to be former free spirits now plugging through the upper echelons of journalism and law. The oldest house here dates from 1780. According to historian Kathleen Sinclair Wood, the area's frame houses and wraparound porches are "reminiscent of small-town America . . . within minutes of central Washington."

Exit Cleveland Park via busy Thirty-fourth Street to Massachusetts Avenue. As you turn left, the vice president's residence since 1977, a white turreted structure on the grounds of the U.S. Naval Observatory, is visible beyond a fence on the right. (Careful: The intersection sees more bike accidents than any other in the city.) Straight ahead is the Naval Observatory itself, with its 125-year-old telescope, used to discover the moons of Mars in 1877, and the Master Clock of the United States, the world's most accurate timepiece.

The scenery gets much more grandiose as you head down Massachusetts Avenue. You pass the embassies of Britain, Brazil, Japan, and Turkey. There are formal gardens, specimen trees, and a statue of Winston Churchill flashing V-for-victory. The latest addition to this diplomatic corridor is a memorial to poet-philosopher Kahlil Gibran. Though lined by stately linden trees, this is not the most inspiring bicycling territory—you ride on a sidewalk on a street clogged with traffic—but it is a fitting end to a tour of Washington at its most cultivated.

Prince William Forest Park

Distance:	13-mile loop
Approximate pedaling time:	1 hour
Terrain:	Rolling hills
Surface:	Well-maintained park roads with no shoulder but little traffic
Things to see:	Reclaimed woodlands
Facilities:	Camping (RVs and tents) with hot showers, picnic grounds, rest rooms
Option:	Mountain biking
Recommended for:	Tourists, Natural Beauty, Countryside

This is a simple, 13-mile ride that's great for getting into shape for longer rides. It includes a 6-mile loop you can ride a few times for a longer workout. You can even switch modes by bringing mountain bikes to ride the 20 miles of fire roads through the dense forest of this unusual National Park.

A few of the fire roads are closed to bikes. Check with the ranger before revving up the stump-jumper. He or she will give you a map showing approved routes. When this was written, routes *not* recommended for biking included the North Orenda Road and Old Pyrite Road. A park spokesperson also warned bikers against riding on the 35 miles of hiking trails. "Our rangers are ready to nab 'em," she said.

There's excellent camping (both tents and trailer hook-ups) should you wish to stay over to spend a second day hiking. Small tent sites are available on a first-come, first-served basis and cost $10. Cabins and larger tent sites can be reserved; call (703) 221–4706 for information. Large groups can stay in one of five rustic camps (accommodating 25 to 40 campers for $30 a night) built by the Civilian

NORTH

234

West Gate Rd.

Scenic Drive

Prince William
Forest Park

95

Quantico
Marine Base

619

Pine Grove Pinic Area
Parking R

START

HOW
to get
there   From Washington, drive south
about 30 miles on Interstate 95.
Take exit 150 at Route 619/Prince
William Forest Park.

DIREC- TIONS for the ride

- From Pine Grove Picnic area, just off Route 619, right toward park entrance.
- Right on Scenic Drive.
- Continue counterclockwise on Scenic Drive. Camping and rest rooms available about halfway through the loop.
- At about mile 9, turn right to head toward park exit.
- Left into Pine Grove Picnic Area.

Conservation Corps (CCC) in the 1930s. The young construction workers milled their wood on site from fallen trees. They were paid $1.00 a day. With unemployment near 25 percent nationally, there were plenty of takers. They also built lakes near each site. Today these rough-hewn cabins, surrounded by forest and built of shingle, iron, and stone, are listed in the National Register of Historic Places.

Originally named Chopawamsic ("by the separation of the outlet"), the 16,000-acre park is a great place to relive history or to study natural history. Even cyclists may spot a wild turkey or white-tailed deer or wend along the edge of a meadow or a stand of Virginia pine.

The park is also an example of environmental restoration. When founded by Scotsmen in the 1700s, this area was second only to New York among New World ports. By the next century pyrite mining had become the area's economic base. Sulphur was extracted from this fool's gold and refined for industrial uses. But by 1933 the centuries of mining and farming had exhausted the land. Siltation clogged Quantico Creek and consigned Dumfries Harbor to oblivion. The federal government bought 17,000 acres and ultimately directed that it be rehabilitated as wilderness. The CCC was assigned to the job, and the labor was imported from tent camps right in Washington. In 1948 Prince William Forest Park was born with another social purpose: to provide inner-city youth with camping facilities. The park is still available to serve that function.

Where once were barren fields are now eighty-nine species of shrubs and trees, including hickory, beech, and mountain laurel. Bisected by many streams and paths, the park looks like a piece of nature preserved in its pristine state. The new-growth forest is home to beaver, red fox, copperhead snakes, and the occasional bald eagle. But there are also remnants of civilization: foundations, orchards, cemeteries, and remains of the old pyrite mine.

The park's function of harboring Prince William County's open space becomes increasingly important as development fans out from Washington with accelerating speed. Right now, the park offers one of the few on-road rides in this book where I can guarantee light traffic and uncluttered scenery. There is a small price to pay: This ride requires an admission pass. A three-day ticket costs $4.00 per carload.

Park officials are experimenting with planting grasses to filter runoff pollution that now seeps into the creeks. They hope that these watercourses will supply potable water in just a few years. If so, hot cyclists will probably be among the first to dunk their heads and drink deeply.

Prince George's Urban Farmland

Distance:	15-mile loop
Approximate pedaling time:	90 minutes
Terrain:	Rolling
Surface:	Country roads, wide shoulder
Things to see:	Rustic farm buildings, fields, ponds, log cabin and creeks
Facilities:	Rest rooms at Goddard Space Flight Center and Agriculture Research Visitor's Center (weekdays)
Option:	Visit Goddard Space Flight Center
Recommended for:	Tourists, Families with children, Natural beauty, Countryside

Just like Prince William Forest Park, the Beltsville Agricultural Research Center provides an oasis of green in a rapidly urbanizing area. Whereas the park offers a pristine look at acres of woodlands, the research center preserves another vanishing landscape: that of the American farm.

As the center says in its own brochure, "From the air, the center looks like a 9-mile-long, 4-mile-wide quilted blanket of green fields, pastures, and orchards." All this can be found only 15 miles northeast of the city. Along with the quiet roads, this makes the center a favorite both for bike racers in training and day-trippers coming from the neighboring University of Maryland.

Located on 7,500 acres in Prince George's County, Maryland, the center was created in 1910 to study better means of soil conservation and animal husbandry. Its nucleus was a 475-acre farm acquired by the federal government at that time. Among the notable results of re-

NORTH

Fort Meade

95

Edmonston Rd.

Visitor's Center ᴿ

National Agricultural Research Ctr.

Powder Mill Rd.

Beaver Dam Rd.

Springfield Rd.

Soil Conservation Rd.

Exit 22

193

★ Park & **START**

Goddard Flight Ctr.
ᴿ

495

HOW
to get
there
From the Washington Beltway (Route 495) drive to Greenbelt exit (Route 193). Take 193 to Soil Conservation Service Road and turn left. In 100 yards, turn left at the light onto Explorer Road. Park at the NASA visitor's center on the left.

DIREC-TIONS for the ride

- From the parking lot at the NASA visitor's center, ride back to the traffic light at Soil Conservation Road (SCS Road), and turn left.
- Head north on SCS Road to Beaver Dam Road; turn right.
- Sharp left on Springfield Road.
- Left on Powder Mill Road. Pass turn-off for Soil Consevation Road on left.
- Look for driveway to log cabin visitor's center on left.
- Left on Edmonston Road.
- In about 0.2 mile, left on Beaver Dam Road.
- Right on SCS Road to return to start.

---

search conducted here are the plump-breasted Thanksgiving turkey (the one the Pilgrims ate was a stringy wild turkey), the "modern hog" (it's leaner and longer than the old-fashioned pig and has an extra vertebra for more chops), the Atlantic potato (good for low-fat chips), and the domestic strawberry. Today the research center is devoted primarily to studies of the environment and global food supplies. It is operated by the U.S. Department of Agriculture, which maintains on the grounds more than 1,000 buildings and thousands of cattle, turkeys, and chickens.

Many of those buildings are of the rustic variety: great wooden silos, rambling, weathered barns, and clapboard farmhouses with sagging front porches. What it amounts to (for the cyclist, at least) is a wide-open space in a region where that's rare. The roads are well-paved. Some have broad, clean shoulders, while others are somewhat narrow.

Particularly when traffic is light early in the morning, the ride is a delight. The loop described in this ride is only a sample—there are other quiet lanes to explore as well. You'll pass ponds, stands of hardwood, pastures full of cows and sheep, a strawberry patch, orchards, old railroad tracks, and two creeks.

The center once looked inward and did not encourage public visitation, but it now encourages both recreation and education. In 1989 the center dedicated a new visitor's center in a restored log cabin, originally modeled after the lodges in Yellowstone National Park. The so-called Log Lodge was built from 1934 to 1937 by the Civilian Conservation Corps (CCC) from timbers 40 to 50 feet long, harvested and milled on site. The CCC also built the major roads through the facility. Until 1985 the lodge was used as a cafeteria, where diners included Dwight D. Eisenhower and Nikita Khrushchev. It stands on Powder Mill Road on the western portion of this route. The restoration cost more than $500,000. Go in to get a map and see the exhibits.

On the way in or out, you can visit the visitor's center at the Goddard Space Flight Center, a NASA research facility with a $1 billion annual budget and 12,000 employees. The museum at the center offers film clips in an eight-screen cinema, a solar telescope for sunspot viewing, an outdoor rocket park, and a simulated space-flight trainer. It's open daily 9:00 A.M. to 4:00 P.M. One-hour-long tours are available every day. The center also hosts model-rocket launches two Sunday afternoons a month. Admission is free. Call (301) 286–8981 for more information.

Two Creeks of Maryland

Distance:	13 miles, one way
Approximate pedaling time:	3 hours
Terrain:	Flat
Surface:	Paved off-road trails with one major intersection
Things to see:	Historic mill, woodlands, suburban neighborhoods
Facilities:	Rest rooms, playgrounds, snack bar at Wheaton Park
Options:	Rock Creek Park, Mormon Temple
Recommended for:	Families with children, Natural beauty, Mostly bike paths, Countryside

When it comes to development of off-road multiuse trails, Prince George's and eastern Montgomery Counties in Maryland are quickly catching up with their neighbors. This ride connects two off-road trails along Sligo Creek Parkway and the Northwest Branch of the Anacostia River, each traversing bucolic parks. They are particularly worth exploring if you live in the area and bicycle with a young family. The quiet, 5-mile-long Northwest Branch is a good venue to graduate youngsters from training wheels.

The ride starts at Montgomery County's Wheaton Regional Park, just 6 miles north of Washington. Look around a bit before you leave. On 496 acres, the park includes a hockey-size, open-air ice rink (I've even cycled to my skating sessions in winter), Brookside Gardens (second only to the National Arboretum in its seasonal floral display), a miniature railway with a brand-new station house, and a merry-go-round.

Wheaton
Regional Park
R

Park &
START

■ ■ ■ Optional Connection
to Rock Creek Park;
Rock Creek Park Trail
(Rides 3 and 4)

NORTH

Stoneybrook
Dr.

Capitol
View Ave.

Sligo Creek Trail

Forest Glen Rd.

495

Beltway

Trail ends

Rock Creek Park Trail

Sligo Creek
Trail

MARYLAND

R

Piney Branch
Ave.

Northwest Branch

Adelphi
Mill R

New
Hampshire
Ave.

Riggs Rd.

D.C.

Erskine
Rd.

R

Chapman Rd.

NW Branch

Trail ends

HOW
to get
there

By auto, take exit 21 from the
Beltway (Route 495) to Georgia
Avenue (Route 97). Turn right on
Arcola Avenue and left on Kemp Mill
Road to park entrance.

DIREC-TIONS for the ride

- Start at Wheaton Regional Park, Orebaugh and Arcola Avenues, Wheaton, Maryland. Ride the loop road around the park.
- Ride south on Sligo hiker/biker trail (off-road).
- Sligo Creek Parkway ends at New Hampshire Avenue. Turn left on New Hampshire and immediately right on Erskine Street.
- Right on Riggs Road (busy).
- Left on Chapman Road.
- Right on Northwest Branch hiker/biker trail (off-road).
- At end of park, turn around and double back.
- Cross Riggs Road to reach historic Adelphi Mill and continue to northern end of park.

Option: Connection to Rock Creek Park in Maryland (2 miles).
- Head south from Wheaton Regional Park as stated above.
- Just before passing under Beltway bridge, turn right on Forest Glen Road.
- At intersection of Seminary Road, turn right on Capitol View Avenue.
- Capitol View becomes Stoneybrook, which ends at Beach Drive (Rock Creek Park).

Option: While on Stoneybrook, turn right into visitor's center for Mormon Temple (see Ride 4).

The off-road trail heads south through quiet suburban neighborhoods and along Sligo Creek Park, which is roughly akin to Rock Creek Park for this area of Maryland. The trail parallels the Sligo Creek Parkway, a two-lane road that winds through some pretty Takoma Park neighborhoods. The motorists are used to seeing cyclists, but take extra care to be safe and visible nonetheless. If you chose to ride on the parkway, be aware that the shoulder is quite narrow, if not nonexistent.

The parkway ends at New Hampshire Avenue, and the bike path takes a temporary detour around an area where bridge repairs are needed. From here an on-road route through neighborhoods will connect you to the restored Adelphi Mill, built in 1790 by two brothers from Pennsylvania (hence "Adelphi"), abandoned in 1850, and restored (albeit not to working condition) in the 1950s. One of the only two surviving grist mills in Prince George's County, it's used today for weddings and meetings.

The mill is located midway through a 5-mile stretch of off-road trail parallel to the Northwest Branch. This tributary of the Anacostia River is well stocked with trout by the U.S. Fish and Wildlife Service. Located just steps away is the miller's cottage, built of fieldstone in 1792 and now leased as a private residence for the county archaeologist.

The ravine is deep and wild-looking, but the path is flat and quiet. There are some mica-covered boulders in the stream, a duck pond, and a portion of streambed full of submerged carbonized logs. These soggy hunks of driftwood are estimated to be more than 120 million years old. If removed from their aquatic state, they would disintegrate.

Like Sligo Creek, this oblong park straddles Prince George's and Montgomery Counties.

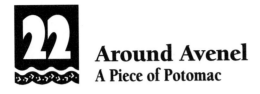

Around Avenel
A Piece of Potomac

Distance:	15 miles
Approximate pedaling time:	90 minutes
Terrain:	Rolling
Surface:	Smooth roads, some with adjacent off-road trails
Things to see:	Stream-cut ravines, meadows, ritzy neighborhoods
Facilities:	PGA golf course, Potomac Village and MacArthur Plaza shopping areas with food, banks, rest rooms
Option:	Visit Great Falls Tavern and Visitor's Center
Recommended for:	Natural beauty, Countryside

Far from my tie-dyed, gritty town of Takoma Park ("where old hippies go to die") lies a land of horse farms and houses the size of small hotels, five-car garages, and home squash courts. It's Potomac, Maryland, the Washington area's own East Egg, and it's threaded with some two-lane blacktop that beckons cyclists. This chapter outlines a figure eight that's a great training ride.

A bit of background. Until 1880, Potomac was called Offutt's Crossroads, named for the area's largest landowners. It remained sleepy and rural until the early part of the century, when some fields were turned into estates. Additional cachet came with the 1924 opening of the Congressional Country Club, followed by the 1930 founding of the Potomac Hunt Club: a squirearchy was born. Potomac residents today are more likely to go golfing or shopping than fox

To Seneca

NORTH

Potomac Village R

River Road (Trail)

Persimmon Tree Rd.

190

191

Bradley Blvd.

Oaklyn Drive

Falls Road (Trail)

To D.C.

Great Falls Park

Clubhouse Road

Oaklyn Drive

Persimmon Tree Road

Equestrian Center

Avenel Visitor's R Center

Park & **START**

Golf Course R

Old Angler's Inn R

Capital Beltway

(Trail)

MacArthur Plaza R

POTOMAC RIVER

MacArthur Blvd.

HOW to get there By car, take Route 495 to River Road West (Exit 39). Turn left on Bradley Boulevard. At four-way stop, go straight to pick up Oaklyn Drive. Turn left on Clubhouse Road. Take first right into equestrian center.

DIREC-TIONS for the ride

- Leave equestrian center via driveway.
- Left on Clubhouse Road.
- At **T** intersection, right on Oaklyn Drive.
- At four-way stop, left on Persimmon Tree Road.
- At oblique **T** intersection, right on River Road (Route 190). Take bike path on left.
- At four-way intersection with traffic light, right on Bradley Boulevard (Route 191).
- At four-way stop, left on Persimmon Tree Road.
- At **T** intersection at bottom of hill, right on MacArthur Boulevard. *Option:* Ride left on MacArthur for 0.4 mile to shops/rest rooms.
- Right on Falls Road.
- Right on Oaklyn Drive.
- Right on Clubhouse Road.
- Right into equestrian center.

hunting, but the area has retained many horse pastures and bridle paths. Equestrian fever still runs high.

Start at Avenel, a 1,000-acre former horse farm that is now a luxury housing development centered around a new 225-acre, professional-circuit golf course. Avenel is packed with visual niceties and amenities: meadows, rows of freshly planted trees, iron lampposts, preserved forests. Even the brass-plated, neo-everything architecture isn't bad by local standards.

Begin in the gravel parking area of the equestrian center, where pastures engulf a fine old timber-frame horse barn. After heading down a short drive, take a right if you want to see the Tournament Players Club, where as many as 32,000 people convene each May to watch the Kemper Open golf tournament. Otherwise, turn left on Clubhouse Road to start the ride.

A right on Oaklyn Drive takes you past the information center (they were nice to me despite my gritty bike clothes), where you can get the scoop on million-dollar homes in eight separate Avenel devel-

opments. The pool-table-smooth road provides entertaining dips and turns, and the scenery is impeccably groomed. Even the meadows of goldenrod and second-growth forests look picked over and arranged. The housing cluster on the right is called Player's Crossing; on the left is Player's Gate. (The developer calls these villages, but if they are, I'm Greg LeMond.)

Turn left on Persimmon Tree Drive and leave Avenel for an older neighborhood of grand ranch houses and Tudors mixed in with new "tract mansions," as Henry Allen of the *Washington Post* dubs Potomac's large new houses. The road surface remains superb. Persimmon Tree winds a bit until you come to a busy, oblique intersection with River Road. Be careful of heavy traffic here. Turn right to stay on this route; turn left if you need refreshments in the Potomac Village shopping area, less than one-third of a mile down River Road. There's a trendy patisserie and gourmet coffee shop as well as a grocery store.

Back on the route, follow River Road east for about 1.5 miles. This is a busy, two-lane arterial, but there's a parallel path for bailing out if you feel uncomfortable in traffic. It's a straight shot past more big homes until you turn right at a traffic light on Bradley Boulevard.

Bradley is more lightly traveled, but there is also an adjacent path available, smooth, albeit narrow. Proceed to a four-way stop at the intersection with Persimmon Tree. Take a left (this is the knot in the figure eight) to explore a new part of Persimmon Tree. You pass another part of Avenel ("Willowgate"), cross the Capital Beltway on an overpass, and descend to the bluffs of the Potomac River. At this midpoint of the ride, if you are in need of refreshment, you can turn left on MacArthur Boulevard to a shopping center with a natural foods store and deli. Now heading west on MacArthur Boulevard, you're riding through a neighborhood mixing older bungalows with newer homes and dense vegetation. On the left you'll pass the Naval Surface Warfare Center, which is a research facility, not a dock or shipyard. What looks like a mile-long Quonset hut is used for testing model ships. Just over the horizon find the Carderock Recreation Area (a mecca for rock-climbers and rappellers), rapids of the Potomac, and islands named Offutt, Turkey, Vaso, Hermit, and Perry.

MacArthur Boulevard is popular for serious cyclists in training. To its credit, Montgomery County has alerted drivers with recently posted SHARE THE ROAD signs. There's also an adjacent off-road trail/shoulder. I'd rather ride the road; stick to the shoulder if you prefer a 10-mph pace, cars bother you, or you're riding with children.

At Old Angler's Inn, follow the road to the right as it begins a mile-long climb through dense woods. There's a nice, wide shoulder along this stretch. The next turn is a right onto Falls Road. You have the option of turning left and descending into Great Falls Park, where you can just explore awhile and return to our route, or pick up the C & O Canal Trail and ride a dozen miles back to Washington. If you're staying with the route be alert, as Falls Road is narrow and crowded. Again, an adjacent trail on the left offers a way out. A right turn on Oaklyn Drive brings you through more of Avenel ("Oaklyn Woods," "Chartwell") through open space set aside for the future water-treatment plant. Just before the open space, look closely for the village of Pleasant Gate. You'll immediately sense this section is quite different from its surroundings. The homes are only one story and attached. These sixty homes were built to provide "moderate income housing," and twenty are still held by the county housing authority for low-income tenants. You can bet the waiting list is long! Stay on Oaklyn until Clubhouse Road, where you can return to the equestrian center's parking area.

To Edwards Ferry

Distance:	23-mile loop
Approximate pedaling time:	2 hours
Terrain:	Mostly flat, some hills
Surface:	Smooth two-lane roads and dirt towpath
Things to see:	Ruins at Edwards Ferry, farm country, wildlife area, swamp, C & O Canal, one-room schoolhouse
Facilities:	Camping, stores at Riley's Lock and pit, en route
Recommended for:	Tourists, Families with children (canal route), Natural beauty, Mostly bike paths, Countryside

This loop explores the Potomac's scenic bottomlands, where a slower, straighter part of the river above Great Falls glides by cornfields, swamps, sod farms, oak forest, and ruins. It's a good ride to append to Ride 24 (Sugarland Loop) or Ride 25 (Escape to the Maryland Countryside), but it also stands well on its own.

Start about 15 miles west of D.C. at the Sycamore Landing parking area of the C & O Canal. This is the land of Seneca sandstone, the building material for the Smithsonian castle and other Washington landmarks. Sycamore Landing is an old canal landing abandoned in 1924 with the rest of the C & O. The canal is dry here and a hardwood forest is overtaking its bed. You can look over the Potomac to Maddox Island.

Ride away from the canal through McKee-Beshers Wildlife Area, which looks like a farm because its lowland fields are sown with corn

NORTH

Poole's Store

Riley's R
Lock Rd.

Partnership Rd.

Seneca
Schoolhouse

Seneca Creek
State Park

River Rd.

POTOMAC RIVER

Hughes Rd.

190

Sycamore
Landing

Park &
START

W. Willard Rd.

River Rd.

R

Sycamore
Landing Rd.

Offutt Rd.

Mt. Nebo Rd.

R C&O Canal Towpath

West
Offutt Rd.

Edward's Ferry Rd.

Edward's
Ferry Lock

HOW
to get
there

Take the Beltway to River Road West (Exit 39).
Follow River Road through Potomac Village. Bear left
at sign for Route 112 to stay on River Road. After passing
Hughes Road on right, take next left on Sycamore Landing
Road (unpaved) and park at the end, next to the C & O Canal.

DIREC-TIONS for the ride

- North (away from canal) on Sycamore Landing Road (unpaved).
- Left on River Road.
- Bear right on Mt. Nebo Road.
- Left on Offutt Road.
- Left on West Offutt Road.
- Left on Edwards Ferry Road.
- Pass Sycamore Landing on towpath.
- Left on Riley's Lock Road.
- Left on River Road (store across street).
- Left on Sycamore Landing Road.

and other plants that attract wildlife. The wildlife attract hunters, so expect gunfire in hunting season. Cross Horsepen Branch on a bridge and turn left on River Road, which becomes Old River Road when it narrows suddenly to one lane and enters the woods. (This was an Indian path later used to roll hogsheads of tobacco to Georgetown.) There's a grade to climb here with a view of a hardwood swamp on the left. I've seen red-tailed hawks perched on the snags of dead sycamores. Be looking for bits of prickly pear clinging to rock outcrops on the right. The cactus is native to the East.

Past a shale rock face, pass through a mile-long lawn—a sod farm. The scenery becomes vaguely British when hedgerows appear, but less so where large homes on five-acre lots have replaced eroded farmland. Several large horse farms and Montgomery County's enlightened rural preservation program have helped save a semblance of countryside. Glide down Edwards Ferry Road past fields once strewn with cobblestones and boulders (this was the prehistoric Potomac's bed when the river was much higher). There are still some rocks in these piedmont fields.

At Edwards Ferry, there's a well-preserved lock house and the stone-and-brick ruins of a grain warehouse. The ferry landing was once a transfer point for wagonloads of grain, coal, and supplies. Across this wide, fairly calm part of the Potomac is Virginia's Goose Creek. Unfortunately, this natural area now sports a golf course.

Pick up the towpath for a return past Sycamore Landing and on to another well-maintained lock named Riley's. The towpath can get pretty muddy along this stretch, but it's not so bad that you would need a mountain bike. There's camping on the canal at Chisel Branch Hiker-Biker Camp (water pumps and outhouse available), but check ahead to see if you need reservations (202–653–5190).

After visiting Riley's Lock, described in Ride 24, follow Riley's Lock Road to River Road, and turn left at Poole's Country Store. Shortly, you'll pass the Seneca Schoolhouse Museum. This one-room schoolhouse was constructed in 1886 of the same locally quarried sandstone used to build the Smithsonian castle. The school was used until 1910, then converted to a private residence until 1981 when the building was restored to its original state. The original wood floors are intact, and some of the original desks remain.

The schoolhouse is open every Sunday from March to December. By appointment, the school is operated as a living classroom, with costumed docents providing a full day of 1880s-style schooling for field trips.

Complete your ride down River Road and back into Sycamore Landing. On my most recent ride, I was pleasantly surprised to see a flock of wild turkeys at this point.

Sugarland Loop

Distance:	13 miles
Approximate pedaling time:	90 minutes
Terrain:	Rolling
Surface:	Well-paved country roads
Things to see:	Old C & O Canal aqueduct, one-room schoolhouse, Homestead Farm (for pick-your-own fruit in season)
Facilities:	Rest rooms at Riley's Lock, food at Poole's Country Store
Recommended for:	Natural beauty, Countryside

Here's one of the sweetest rides in Montgomery Country—a little corner of road cycling heaven within forty-five minutes of downtown Washington. The Sugarland Loop lies in the county's northwest corner, long a favorite destination for area cyclists. You'll be likely to run into group rides organized by the Potomac Pedalers Club or training rides organized by any of the several local racing clubs.

The Sugarland Loop is a perfect 13-mile jaunt. For a longer ride, combine it with Ride 23 (To Edwards Ferry). For a *really* long ride, try Ride 25 (Escape to the Maryland Countryside), which covers some of the same roads.

Start at Riley's Lock, off River Road just west of Seneca Road. The parking lot here provides a convenient staging area not only for cyclists but also for hikers heading out on the C & O Canal towpath, for picnickers using the grassy park on the river, and for boaters putting in at Seneca Creek for easy access to the Potomac. Be sure to take a look at the aqueduct, which used to carry the canal *over* Seneca Creek on its way west. Its huge blocks of Seneca sandstone still arch over

POOLESVILLE

HOW to get there

Take the Beltway to River Road West (Exit 39). Follow River Road through Potomac Village. Turn left at sign for Route 112 to stay on River Road. Then, at bottom of long hill, turn left onto Riley's Lock Road. Park in lot at end of road.

White's Ferry Rd.

Homestead Farm

Sugarland Rd.

Hughes Rd.

Sugarland Rd.

Partnership Rd.

Polo Grounds

Montevideo Rd.

River Rd.

Seneca Schoolhouse

Old River Rd.

Poole's Country Store

Seneca Creek State Park

Riley's Lock Rd.

Seneca Rd.

POTOMAC RIVER

River Rd.

Park & **START**

NORTH

DIREC-TIONS for the ride

- From start/finish at Riley's Lock parking area, ride away from river on Riley's Lock Road.
- Left on River Road.
- Right on Partnership Road in about a mile.
- Follow Partnership Road to end, crossing Sugarland Road en route.
- Right on White's Ferry Road.
- Right on Sugarland Road at cluster of small houses. Ride carefully, as Sugarland narrows to a single lane of concrete slab roadway with dirt shoulders.
- Pass Homestead Farm, a favorite pick-your-own destination, on the right.
- Left on Montevideo Road.
- Left on Old River Road just before Montevideo ends at (new) River Road.
- Left on River Road at Poole's Country Store.
- Immediate right on Riley's Lock Road to return to parking area.

the wide creek, but the canal dried up along here years ago.

Ride back toward River Road along Riley's Lock Road, which provides a nice creek-side warm-up. Then turn west onto River Road, shortly passing by the Seneca Schoolhouse Museum, described in Ride 23. Keep an eye out for your right turn onto Partnership Road.

Partnership Road is a cyclist's dream road—few cars, lined by woods and horse farms, a polo club, very few houses and driveways, just one intersection, just a couple of hills. Nothing could be simpler or nicer.

Then, make a sharp right onto White's Ferry Road. This is also a beautiful stretch of roadway, but more heavily traveled.

Turn right after a few miles onto Sugarland Road. You'll soon pass by Homestead Farm, which helps keep this area's agricultural tradition alive by offering pick-your-own fruits and vegetables from late

May (strawberries) through October (pumpkins). If you'd like to sample the farm's offerings, make a quick detour up the driveway. The owners operate a small stand where you can buy already-picked produce. If you stop, there are picnic tables to enjoy your purchases.

Soon after Homestead Farm, turn left onto Montevideo Road. You'll dive down a short hill, cross a one-lane bridge, then climb up the other side on your way to another of this area's country institutions. Poole's Country Store, located on Old River Road toward the end of this ride, is a favorite all-purpose stop. You can refill your water bottle, buy a soda or cup of coffee, pick up a sandwich, catch up on the latest community news, or just sit on the front stoop and reflect on a perfect 13-mile ride.

For a Workout:
Escape to the Maryland Countryside

Distance:	40- or 58-mile loop
Approximate pedaling time:	3 or 5 hours
Terrain:	Very hilly
Surface:	Suburban and country roads
Things to see:	Horse farms, fields, historic Poolesville, Maryland, Sugarloaf Mountain, Potomac riverfront
Options:	18-mile round-trip ride to Sugarloaf Mountain; end-of-ride return to Metrorail station
Facilities:	Poole's Store, Poolesville, Potomac
Recommended for:	Natural beauty, Countryside, Workout

This is a route suggested by a person who knows more about biking than almost anyone around the Beltway: Mike Dornfield, a former associate bicycling coordinator for Washington, D.C.

Mike developed the route as a weekend getaway, but I've adapted it as a ride from Metrorail's Red Line through the inner suburbs of Montgomery County, with a destination of the quiet country town of Poolesville, a Civil War site of minor importance. On the way out and the way back you bisect the tony community of Potomac, Maryland, where the huge houses are likely to be augmented by a horse barn and a steeplechase course. The ride concludes with a historic section of the Potomac River before ending in Georgetown. The optional return will lead you back to the Metro if you parked there.

Start at Metrorail's Grosvenor Station. (This commencement point may also be reached by riding through Rock Creek Park, as described in Rides 3 and 4.) The immediate area is strictly suburban blah, with a six-lane road and ramps dominating the scenery. But a nifty subur-

Park &
START

Grosvenor
Metro

Rockville Pike

355

To Georgetown
Fletcher's Boats

Tuckerman Ln.

Cabin John
Regional Park

Arizona Ave.

Canal Rd.

MacArthur Blvd.

C & O Canal
Towpath

R
Persimmon Tree Rd.

Falls Rd.

Glen Rd.

Query
Mill
Rd.

Esworthy Rd.

Seneca Rd.

Westerly Ave.

R
Montevideo Rd.

POTOMAC RIVER

Fisher Ave.

Sugarland
Rd.

Hughes Rd.

River Rd.

POOLESVILLE
R

White's Ferry Rd.

West Willard Rd.

NORTH

HOW
to get
there

By auto, take the Beltway to exit 34; take Route 355
North to Grosvenor Station. By Metro, Red Line to
Grosvenor. By bike, take path through Rock Creek Regional
Park in Maryland to Route 355, turn right and right again onto
Tuckerman Lane (loops around Metro station to head west).

DIREC-TIONS for the ride

- From Grosvenor Station, Red Line of Metrorail, take east ramp out of station to Tuckerman Lane. Turn left to head west.
- Cross Route 355 (traffic light) to continue on Tuckerman.
- Take Tuckerman past camping area and Cabin John Regional Park.
- Left on Falls Road.
- First right on Glen Road. Stay on Glen for almost 10 miles.
- At **T** intersection, turn left, downhill, onto Query Mill Road.
- After quick, brisk descent, turn right on Esworthy Road.
- At **T** intersection, left on Seneca Road (Route 112).
- Continue straight as Seneca Road merges with River Road.
- In several miles, right on Montevideo Road (just past Poole's Country Store, a good pit stop).
- At four-way intersection, left on Sugarland Road (*not* Sugarland Lane).
- At **T** intersection, right on Hughes Road.
- Take Hughes Avenue into town of Poolesville.
- Left on Fisher Road; becomes White's Ferry Road in Poolesville.
- Left on West Willard Road (near high school).
- After steep descent, left on River Road.
- Turn right with River Road as Seneca Road continues straight. (To avoid drastic hills and fast traffic on this next stretch of River Road, see "Return option" below.)
- Stay on River Road (use shoulder) through town of Potomac.
- After main intersection of town of Potomac, right on Persimmon Tree Road.
- In several miles (all downhill), left on MacArthur Boulevard. Return to Washington via Cabin John and Glen Echo.
- Back in Washington, right on Arizona Avenue N.W.
- Left on Canal Road near railroad bridge.
- Hard right at entrance to Fletcher's Boat House (canoe rental, refreshments, and fishing gear available).
- Take towpath of C & O Canal to Georgetown, where ride ends.

Mid-ride option (18-mile trip to Sugarloaf Mountain):

- In Poolesville, left on Fisher Avenue (Route 107).
- In 2 miles, right on Wasche Road.
- In 2.5 miles, right on Martinsburg Road.
- Left on Dickerson Road at Darnestown Road.
- In Dickerson, immediate right after bridge on unmarked Mount Ephraim Road; ride 2.5 miles, cross Barnesville Road, and enter Sugarloaf preserve.
- Backtrack via Mount Ephraim to Barnesville Road.
- Left on Barnesville Road.
- Right on Peach Tree Road.
- Left on Route 28 and immediately right on Cattail Road.
- Right on Fisher Avenue in Poolesville.

Return options: To avoid hilliest stretch of River Road, continue straight onto Seneca Road at point where River Road turns right past entrance to Bretton Woods Recreation Center. Retrace route along Esworthy, Query Mill, and Glen Roads to Falls Road. Turn right on Falls Road, then left on River Road to continue ride to Georgetown. Or turn left on Falls Road and pick up Tuckerman Lane back to Grosvenor Metro.

---

ban road called Tuckerman Lane will soon whisk you away from all that. Although not designated a bike route, Tuckerman easily accommodates two wheelers. After starting off with four surprisingly quiet lanes going through an area of condominium apartments, it narrows to two lanes but with a shoulder wide enough for a fire truck.

The scenery is split levels and driveways as far as the eye can see, but traffic remains fairly light, and many of the yards are planted with azaleas and flowering trees. Soon you bisect the creek ravine that contains Cabin John Regional Park, which includes a petting zoo, a 1-mile minature railroad, and seven primitive campsites. At Falls Road, just past a nursery, you run into a row of small farmsteads with

graceful old houses and barns, but don't be fooled—you're not in the country yet. Falls Road winds through the countrified estates of upper Potomac, where the squirearchy have maintained a semblance of the farmscape for horse pastures.

The real country kicks in just past 5,000-acre Seneca Creek State Park at the town of Seneca. From here you can traverse roads lined with wildflowers and high meadows overlooking the Potomac, then huff and puff uphill through real horse farms until reaching the town of Poolesville, which was contested during the Civil War. Founded in 1793 by the merchant John Poole, Poolesville has remained a country town despite some recent development. There's a twenty-building historic district and several antiques shops worth visiting along its tree-lined streets.

The ride downhill from Poolesville has got to be one of the greatest delights in all of cycling. It's an almost vertical descent on a winding country road with pastures and creeks and woods and dancing figures of Queen Anne's lace creeping up to its edge. On the horizon you can sense the valley floor and the surging Potomac, while the foothills of the Blue Ridge Mountains rise into Virginia on the far side. It would be a wonderful place to watch the sun set, framed by streaking clouds and golden grasses and grains, if you didn't have many more miles to ride before dark.

Back on River Road, be prepared for more pretty scenery as you pass polo grounds, a wildlife management area, and a state park. After Riley's Lock Road, River Road turns right and subjects you to some drastic hills, and increasing traffic on the way through forests and then more estates of Potomac. Pass through Potomac's clogged center, then turn right on Persimmon Tree Drive to return to Washington via MacArthur Boulevard—a route described in Ride 10.

An optional return route avoids this last stretch of River Road *and* gives you the further option of returning to your starting point at the Grosvenor Metro. After passing Riley's Lock Road, simply continue straight on Seneca Road as River Road turns right. Retrace your route along Esworthy, Query Mill, Glen, Falls, and Tuckerman Roads back to the Grosvenor station.

An optional ride from Poolesville takes you to the Washington area's only "mountain"—1,280-foot Sugarloaf Mountain, a National Historic Landmark surrounded by a 3,000-acre, privately owned preserve. Sugarloaf has been called "an outpost of the Appalachians." During the Civil War, Union troops used this precipice to observe General Robert E. Lee fording the Potomac at White's Ferry en route to Antietam Battlefield. Feeling really hardy? Ride to Sugarloaf's peak before turning back and enjoy the tremendous views.

For a Workout:
The Three-State Special

Distance:	57-mile loop
Approximate pedaling time:	6 hours
Terrain:	Hilly
Surface:	Back roads and two-laners with wide shoulders
Things to see:	Antietam Battlefield, Harpers Ferry National Historic Park, farmland
Recommended for:	Tourists, Natural beauty, Countryside, Workout

If all cyclists were like David Brown, books like this would never be published. Mr. Brown, a Washington lawyer, owns a weekend house in Round Hill, Virginia, 5 miles from the end of the W & OD Trail. With a detailed Virginia map in hand, he started creating his own bike routes that include historic and scenic areas of Virginia, West Virginia, and Maryland. My great thanks to him for sharing his two favorites, which I've combined here into one long ride.

Many of the roads are quiet and little traveled. Just to the west is an apple-growing region. The busier routes feature wide shoulders. The two Potomac crossings can be made on safe bridges. By turning around at South Mountain Natural Area in Maryland, you can shave about one-fifth the distance from the ride.

The ride cuts a swath between the Blue Ridge and Short Hill Mountains. It also takes you through the towns of Hillsboro, Virginia; Sharpsburg, Maryland; Brunswick, Maryland; and Lovettsville, Virginia. As a bicyclist, you'll appreciate riding through Hillsboro, where a historical marker notes this is the birthplace of Susan Koerner Wright, mother of bicycle builders and pioneer aviators Wilbur and

NORTH

BOONESBORO, MD
R

34

67S

ANTIETAM

Burnside Br. Rd.

SHARPSBURG,
MD R

Trego Rd.

MARYLAND

John
Brown's
Farm

POTOMAC
RIVER

C & O CANAL

WEST VIRGINIA

67

HARPERS FERRY, W. VA

3
340

340

478
180

17

LOUDOUN
HEIGHTS

BRUNSWICK,
MD R

SHENANDOAH RIVER

673

287

POTOMAC
RIVER

671

690

WEST VIRGINIA

9

VIRGINIA

HILLSBORO, VA
R

VIRGINIA

690

W & OD
Trail

LEESBURG, VA →

Park &
★ START

ROUND HILL

7

PURCELLVILLE, VA

HOW to get there
By bicycle, take W & OD Trail to end at Purcellville. By auto, take Route 7 west.

DIREC-TIONS for the ride

Note: Follow directions for Sharpsburg section carefully, as not every small street is shown on the map.

■ From Twenty-first Street in Purcellville (end of W & OD Trail), head north on Route 690.

■ Near town of Hillsboro, Route 690 comes to a **T**. Turn left on Route 9.

■ Second right onto Route 671.

■ Head north to Loudoun Heights, Virginia. Cross Potomac on bridge. Road merges with Route 340 in Maryland (four lanes with wide shoulders). Right on Route 340 north.

Optional trip to Harpers Ferry, West Virginia:

Left on 340 to historical park (about 2 miles). Double back to rejoin ride at Route 67.

■ Bear right off Route 340 to Route 67 toward Boonesboro.

■ Pass by towns of Garretts Mill, August, Yarrowsburg, and Gapland, to South Mountain Natural Area.

■ Left on Trego Road (becomes Mt. Briar Road).

■ **Optional trip to John Brown's Farm.** Left at marker to Kennedy Farm, John Brown's home. Return to route. Nine miles round–trip.

■ Left on Porterstown Road.

■ At **T** intersection, left on Route 34 (busy with shoulder).

■ Ride through town of Sharpsburg; right on Route 65.

■ Right off Route 65 to battlefield visitor's center. *Option:* 8.5-mile tour of battlefield (details at visitor's center).

■ From visitor's center, left on Route 65.

■ Left on Route 34, through Keedysville.

■ Ride into town of Boonesboro. At traffic light, right on Alternate Route 40 east.

■ Right on Route 67 south.

■ Take Route 67 to Route 340. Turn left to head east.

■ Right on Route 180. Bear right onto Route 487.

■ Just before the bridge, turn left on Virginia Avenue, then immediate right on West B Street.

- At flashing light, right on Route 17 and cross bridge over Potomac to Virginia (Route 17 becomes Route 287 south).
- Right on Route 673.
- Left on Route 690.
- Near Hillsboro, right on Route 9.
- Left on Route 690 to Purcellville.

Orville Wright. Located in Washington County, Brunswick was once a thriving railroad town, with more than 1,300 people working for the B & O system. Much of its gritty heritage survives, along with a few trains carrying commuters to Washington. Its old houses are arranged in a cozy grid in the shadow of the Catoctin Mountains.

Not far from David Brown's weekend retreat, the area around the confluence of the Shenandoah and the Potomac Rivers was hotly contested during the Civil War. Abolitionist John Brown's raid on Harpers Ferry helped precipitate the conflict. In 1862 Stonewall Jackson captured the town, much to the embarrassment of Abraham Lincoln. Today most of the town has been preserved as a national park, with shops and historical exhibits installed in the old buildings. Founded in 1733, the town offers views of the surrounding rivers and mountains. (Thomas Jefferson called the vista of the two rivers meeting "one of the most stupendous scenes in nature.")

If you take the detour to visit historic Harpers Ferry, you also might be attracted by the markers on Trego Road toward John Brown's farm, Kennedy Farmhouse. Recently restored by the National Park Service, this is the site where Brown and others collected arms and ammunition for months prior to their raid on the arsenal in 1859.

Just to the north, Antietam National Battlefield Park commemorates the war's bloodiest day of fighting. On September 17, 1862, some 23,000 of the blue and gray soldiers were killed or wounded. The battle ended in a draw, with the Southerners denied the tactical victory they hoped would end the war. The 6.5-mile one-way loop around the park is perfect for cyclists—providing they are feeling reverent. The last time I was there, a group of Civil War re-enactors, authentically dressed down to their eyeglasses, were solemnly setting up camp and preparing artillery as though they were about to charge into battle. They were living in old canvas tents and stoking pit fires, for this was November.

Other highlights of an Antietam tour include the West Woods, where Union forces lost 2,200 troops in thirty minutes; the homespun Dunker Church on disputed high ground; and Bloody Lane, no explanation needed. On the much less grisly side, you can turn off Route 65 for a visit to the Piper Farmhouse, General Longstreet's Headquarters during the battle. The 1843 log structure was recently restored as a bed & breakfast with kitchen privileges and reasonable rates. Staying overnight (301–797–1862) will give you more time to explore the upper reaches of the C & O Canal and, just across the river, the college burg of Shepardstown, West Virginia, which once thrived on mills and now thrives on antiques.

Antietam's historic sites are all mixed in with private farms and houses. This has caused some alarm, as preservationists charge that development will ruin this hallowed ground. So the battle for Antietam Creek has not been decided yet.

This is the halfway point on this long ride, and you might have worked up a cyclist's appetite before your return. As you ride on Route 34 through Keedysville, you will pass a favorite carbo-loading spot of local cyclists, the Red Byrd Restaurant. Be sure to order a slice of fresh fruit pie—you've earned it!

The region is fewer than 60 miles from central Washington, D.C., but at times it seems several worlds away. At least once a year the Potomac Area Chapter of American Youth Hostels sponsors guided rides out to Harpers Ferry. It's the easiest way I know of to cycle through three states in one day.

Hardly Hilly Hunt Country Tour

Distance:	31 miles
Approximate pedaling time:	3 hours
Terrain:	Rolling
Surface:	Paved two-lane roads
Things to see:	Historic Middleburg, horse farms, Pot House
Facilities:	Stores in Middleburg, Atoka
Recommended for:	Tourists, Natural beauty, Countryside, Workout

The historic small town of Middleburg is the center of Virginia's Hunt Country, one of the most beautiful cycling spots I know. The natural splendor of this area and an interest in the equestrian life have drawn many of America's privileged to call this home. Current and former residents include philanthropist Paul Mellon, actor Robert Duvall, television personality Willard Scott, diplomats Averill and Pamela Harriman, General George S. Patton, and Redskins owner Jack Kent Cooke. President and Jacqueline Kennedy built their home, Wexford, nearby. Wexford was later rented to Ronald and Nancy Reagan by the then current owner while they awaited the Inauguration. All this means is that we have an extraordinarily beautiful area to enjoy, simply for the pedaling effort!

Middleburg is so small that it has only *one* stoplight, in front of the Red Fox Inn—the oldest, continuously operated inn in America. Founded by Joseph Chinn in 1731, the "ordinary" provided respite for horseback travelers. In 1747, a young surveyor, George Washington, stayed at the Red Fox when employed by Lord Fairfax to survey the surrounding lands. For years, the town was known as Chinn's

NORTH

Mountville Rd.   MOUNTVILLE

745   **733**

St. Louis Rd.   Snickersville Pike

611   **734**

Foxcroft School Rd.

626

Sam Fred Rd.

ATOKA   **748**   **50**

713   **50**   Park &
START ★

Atoka Rd.   MIDDLEBURG

RECTORTOWN   Zulla Rd.

709

710   Rock Hill Mill/
Frogtown Rd.   **702**

Rectortown Rd.

HOW
to get
there
Take Route 66 west to Route
50 (exit 57). Follow Route 50
for approximately 20 miles to town
of Middleburg. Turn right at only
stoplight onto Route 626, Foxcroft Road.
Park in elementary school lot.

DIRECTIONS for the ride

- Left out of school lot.
- Right on Route 50 through Middleburg.
- Left on Zulla Road, Route 709.
- Right on 702, Rock Mill Hill Road (easy to miss).
- Bear left on 710; becomes Frogtown Road.
- At T intersection, right on 710, Rectortown Rd.
- Right on Atoka Road, Route 713.
- Right on Route 50 (shoulder).
- Left at St. Louis Road, Route 611.
- Right on Foxcroft School Road, Route 626.
- Left on Route 745, Mountville Road.
- Bear right onto Route 733.
- In Mountville, right onto Route 734, Snickersville Pike.
- Bear right to remain on Snickersville Pike at Route 773.
- Right on Sam Fred Road, Route 748.
- Right on Route 50 (busy, stay right).
- Right at stoplight back to school parking lot.

Crossing, but it was renamed Middleburgh (the *h* was later dropped) by Leven Powell in 1787, reflecting the fact that the town was halfway between Alexandria and Winchester, the Shenandoah town then at the edge of the western frontier.

Your first stop might be the Pink House, the visitor's center on Madison Street. They can provide you with a walking tour brochure featuring many of the important houses and churches built in the eighteenth and nineteenth centuries. After your bike ride, I suggest you walk around Middleburg and especially to Sharon Cemetery, a peaceful and contemplative place where Union and Confederate soldiers are buried side-by-side.

First, a note about the cycling in this area, and this ride in particular. Virginia Hunt Country is not flat; it is rolling to hilly. Few hills are long, but some can be steep. A "granny gear" is standard equipment for many local cyclists. But, believe me, it's worth the added effort to ride in these parts. Every weekend cyclists can be seen on most of these roads. I put this ride together because so many of my friends wanted to ride in Hunt/Horse Country but were concerned that it was too hilly. This ride takes the least hilly roads I could link together. It's not flat, just "hardly hilly."

Be sure to take an extra water bottle; the little country stores that used to dot this area have been closing rapidly. Ride away from Middleburg westward on Route 50, also known as the John S. Mosby Highway. You'll be riding toward Mount Defiance on the same route Union troops took into the Battle of Middleburg in July 1863. Turn left on Zulla Road, where you'll pass the first of many horse farms. Off to the right, you'll have sweeping views of the Blue Ridge Mountains. In spring, dogwoods and redbud are plentiful along this road; in the fall, the foliage colors are stunning.

Along the Atoka Road, you'll pass Kent Farms, the residence and horse stables of the late Jack Kent Cooke, owner of the Redskins football team. Nearby, the Kent Polo Grounds can be found off Route 624 where polo is played every Sunday afternoon during summer months. Shortly, you'll pass Atoka Farms, a previous estate of Senator John Warner. Cross busy Route 50 and continue on St. Louis Road past Notre Dame Academy. Once a private school for young ladies from wealthy families, it is now coeducational and has a more egalitarian student body.

When you reach the intersection of Foxcroft and Mountville Roads, notice the house off to your right just down Pothouse Road. Known as The Pot House, pottery for local farmers was made here for nearly a century after 1795. As you ride along Mountville Road (one of my favorites) be on the lookout for white-tail deer or a red fox. I rarely come down this road without sighting one or the other. The ride ends with an easy ride down Sam Fred Road, intersecting with busy Route 50. Be sure to stay to the right on Route 50; the trucks and cars should be slowing down as they approach Middleburg, but they still can be quite fast.

Winery and Woods

Distance:	28 miles
Approximate pedaling time:	3 hours
Terrain:	Hilly
Surface:	Paved two-lane roads
Things to see:	Middleburg, wineries
Facilities:	Stores in Middleburg; rest rooms at wineries
Recommended for:	Tourists, Natural beauty, Countryside, Workout

This ride also begins at Middleburg, described in Ride 27. The Civil War left many marks on Middleburg and surrounding villages. Its proximity to Washington placed it where guerrilla actions by Confederate troops frequently occurred. These were the stomping grounds of General John S. Mosby, the "Gray Ghost." The townspeople voted unanimously for secession, sympathized with the Southern Cause, and provided food, shelter, and hiding places for many of Mosby's Rangers. It is said that Mosby himself was hidden for several days in a house still standing on the eastern edge of town, while Union troops searched unsuccessfully as the owners steadfastly denied knowing his whereabouts. The town's residents paid dearly for their allegiance, however; Union troops frequently took horses and other provisions whenever needed—and hauled the few remaining men off to prison in Washington.

The only major battle fought here was about a mile out of town, the Battle of Middleburg. General J.E.B. Stuart was informed that Union troops were traveling westward on Little River Turnpike (now Route 50) toward Ashby's Gap. Initially, he sought to hold them back at Aldie, but he was unsuccessful and fell back to Mount Defiance

NORTH

Snickersville Pike

Mountville Rd.

733

Pothouse Rd.

145

POTHOUSE

Foxcroft School Rd.

Sam Fred Rd.

734

626

748

★ Park &
START

MIDDLEBURG

50

Landmark School Rd.

176

626

Piedmont
Vineyards
R

The Plains Rd.

629

686

Meredyth
Vineyards
R

Landmark Rd.

Halfway

628

679

HOW
to get
there
Take Route 66 west to Route
50 (exit 57). Follow Route 50
for approximately 20 miles to town
of Middleburg. Turn right at only
stoplight onto Route 626, Foxcroft Road.
Park in elementary school lot.

DIRECTIONS for the ride

- Left from parking lot to Route 50 stoplight.
- Right on Route 50 through Middleburg.
- Left on The Plains Road, Route 626.
- Hard left at Halfway onto Landmark Road.
- Bear left TRO [To Remain on] Landmark at Route 679.
- Optional tour of Meredyth Vineyards on left.
- Left TRO Landmark Road at Route 629.
- Left on Landmark School Road, Route 776.
- Cross Route 50 at stoplight.
- Straight onto Foxcroft Road, past starting point.
- Bear right TRO Foxcroft Road at Snake Hill.
- Right on Mountville Road, Route 745.
- Bear right onto Route 733, Mountville Road.
- In Mountville, right onto Route 734, Snickersville Pike.
- Bear right to remain on Snickersville Pike at Route 773.
- Right on Sam Fred Road, Route 748.
- Right on Route 50 (busy, stay right).
- Right at stoplight back to school parking lot.

just outside Middleburg for another stand. Both sides lost many men, but the Union army was eventually successful and went on to capture Upperville and Ashby's Gap. Nearly 2,000 men were lost between the armies; many are buried together in Sharon Cemetery.

Middleburg was largely impoverished after the Civil War, with crops destroyed, horses taken, few able men, and no money to hire farmhands. Houses and farms deteriorated, but fortunately were not destroyed. As the fortunes of Americans grew, they sought open fields for their estates and their newfound interest in horses and foxhunting. The vast, rolling terrain provided the perfect environment for these sports—and for grapes.

Wine has been produced in America since Colonial times. The Virginia General Assembly sought to encourage a native wine industry by its "Act for the Encouragement of the Making of Wine" in 1769, but poor luck in the vineyards and the Revolution interrupted efforts. In the nineteenth century, wine production again flourished in Virginia after a local variety, named Norton after its discoverer, was found to survive. Then came Prohibition, all but terminating the industry.

Viniculture slowly recovered in the mid-twentieth century. American and French vines were grafted together to combine the finesse of vinifera wines with the hardiness and resistance to phylloxera of the native species. By the 1970s, viticultural research and development had made commercial farm wine production possible in Virginia. The first to do so was the Meredyth Vineyards, located just south of Middleburg. They first planted in 1972 and had their first harvest in 1975. Mrs. Thomas Elizabeth Furness started the first commercial vineyard in Virginia since Colonial times at Piedmont Vineyards in 1973, also just south of Middleburg. This bicycle tour takes you by both vineyards, then adds another loop through wonderful, wooded territory north of town.

As this is a figure-eight tour, you could take either loop first. I'd suggest that you first ride the southern one as it is hillier and you'll be less tempted to call it a day when you loop back through Middleburg for the second loop. Ride west through Middleburg, and head south on The Plains Road. This is the same road where Union and Confederate cavalries clashed. You are at a high point now, and the views right and left are spectacular. After cruising downhill, you'll encounter Piedmont Vineyards, with its stately mansion, Waverly, prominently facing the road. Tours and tastings are available most days (540–687–5528).

Don't linger there long, however. You have several more miles of countryside to enjoy, as well as another winery. Continue on The Plains Road to Halfway, so named because it was the midpoint between Middleburg and The Plains, where the train stopped. As you ride up Landmark Road, look for the sign to Meredyth Vineyard on your left. It's down a gravel Road that is rideable on all but the skinniest of tires. After visiting Meredyth Vineyards (540–687–6277), return to Landmark Road and continue the loop back to Middleburg.

You'll return to Middleburg's stoplight; cross over Route 50 past your starting point, and head north on Foxcroft Road . Turn right at The Pot House, described in Ride 27, along Mountville Road, canopied by trees in many places. At Snickersville Turnpike, which is a Virginia Scenic Byway, turn right, passing stables and stone fences through winding, wooded Roads. Be alert for deer here; I've had a few close calls with those bounding whitetails along this Road. Now, circle back to Middleburg, pick up your car, and drive back to the winery you most enjoyed to pick up a few bottles!

Blue Ridge Splendor

Distance:	38 miles
Approximate pedaling time:	3 hours
Terrain:	Rolling to hilly
Surface:	Paved two-lane roads
Things to see:	Views of Blue Ridge Mountains, stables
Facilities:	Stores in Middleburg, Bloomfield
Recommended for:	Tourists, Natural beauty, Countryside, Workout

The Blue Ridge Mountains lie to the west, creating a challenge for cyclists wishing to ride to the Shenandoah Valley. This ride takes us westward far enough to enjoy the mountains' spectacular beauty without tackling their inclines. This ride is particularly colorful in the fall, but I enjoy riding it any time of the year. In fact, it's my favorite ride in the Virginia Hunt Country.

Part of the Appalachians, the Blue Ridge Mountains are some of the oldest eastern mountains. Geologists now believe they once were much larger; towering higher than the Rockies eons ago. However, thousands of years of rain, wind, ice, and weathering smoothed the once snow-capped peaks to today's rolling ridges. The dense hardwood forests provide great hiking opportunities and beautiful foliage. From afar, the mountains are striking as the sunlight, cloud shadows, and haze create unending variations of panoramic display.

Along the way, you'll pass several points of interest reflecting the residents' long-standing interest in horses, including foxhunting, horse shows, racing, and polo. Riding north on Foxcroft Road, you'll pass Glenwood Park, where both point-to-point and steeplechase races are run. Yes, there are differences between the two: largely whether timber or brush fences are to be jumped, whether professionals are allowed to compete, and the size or absence of a purse. However, efforts to make the races more accessible for spectators have tended to limit the rambling point-to-points to a smaller field, making them more like a steeplechase. For most, either will be equally enjoyable, especially if you just happen to ride by as one is under way.

After passing Glenwood Park, you'll go down a fairly steep hill. About midway, on the left, notice the metal sign featuring a fox. This is the home of the Middleburg Hunt; you may hear the baying of foxhounds in the distance. Don't worry, I've never been chased by a pack of hounds on this road. Foxhunting was brought to America by the British, perhaps as long ago as the late 1600s. Unlike opossums or squirrels, foxes are crafty and put up quite a chase. Foxes were so important to expanding the sport, they were imported from England so that they could mix with the indigenous breed and expand their numbers. In America, the fox is rarely killed; the chase is the sport, requiring excellent horsemanship, good hounds, and a well-trained mount.

After turning south at Airmont, you'll have the Blue Ridge Mountains on your right for several miles. Periodically glance over and see how they change as the sunlight shifts. As you cross Route 50, you'll be at Grafton Farm, site of the Upperville Colt and Horse Show, the nation's oldest horse show. Since 1853, interrupted only during war years, this show has featured young colts and fillies, usually raised nearby. While the show was founded to encourage production of top breeding stock, other classes have been added over the years to round out horsemen's interests. The show has grown so much that events now last the first full week of June and occupy fields on both sides of Route 50. The High Jump became a major attraction and, recently, commercialism has taken hold with the Michelob-Upperville Jumper Classic, featuring a very sizable purse.

On Rokeby Road, you'll pass the estate of philanthropist Paul Mellon. Shortly after passing the airstrip on your right, look left and you'll see the roofline of the stables. This is the home of some of Vir-

AIRMONT

NORTH

Airmont Rd.

734

719

Snickersville Pike

BLOOMFIELD

St. Louis Rd.

611

Green Garden Rd.

Blue Ridge Mountains

Millville Rd.

743

Foxcroft School Rd.

Willisville Rd.

623

Upperville
Horse Show

50

626

★

Park &
START

Rokeby Rd.

623

Zulla Rd

710

709

Rectortown Rd.

Frogtown Rd. 702

RECTORTOWN

Rock Hill
Mill Rd.

HOW
to get
there

Take Route 66 west to Route
50 (exit 57). Follow Route 50
for approximately 20 miles to town
of Middleburg. Turn right at only
stoplight onto Route 626, Foxcroft Road.
Park in elementary school lot.

DIREC-TIONS
for the ride

- Right out of school lot onto Foxcroft Road.
- Straight at Pot House Road.
- Right on Route 611, St. Louis Road.
- Left at blinking light, Route 734.
- Left on Airmont Road, Route 719.
- Airmont Road becomes Green Garden Road.
- Left on Millville Road, Route 743.
- Bear right, Route 623, Willisville Road.
- Left on Route 50 (traffic).
- Right on Route 623, Rokeby Road.
- Left at T on Rectortown Road, Route 710.
- Left at T on Zulla Road, Route 709.
- Bear right still on Route 702; becomes Rock Hill Mill Road.
- Left at T on Zulla Road, Route 709.
- Right on Route 50.
- Left at stoplight back to parking lot.

ginia's best thoroughbreds. In addition to the real horseflesh, these stables contain life-size bronze statues of "Mill Reef" and Kentucky Derby winner "Sea Hero." Completing the loop, you'll ride through Rectortown and pass close by yet another horse-oriented sport venue, the Kent Polo Field, on your left down graveled Crenshaw Road. Polo is played here every Sunday afternoon during the summer. If horses really interest you, you might want to take in the annual Stable Tour, held every Memorial Day weekend, when you can visit Rokeby as well as other private stables and stud farms.

To the Races

Distance:	34 miles
Approximate pedaling time:	3 hours
Terrain:	Rolling to hilly
Surface:	Paved two-lane Road s
Things to see:	Great Meadow, The Plains
Facilities:	Stores in Middleburg and The Plains
Recommended for:	Tourists, Natural beauty, Countryside, Workout

This ride takes you to the site of Virginia's premier steeplechase event, The Virginia Gold Cup. Along the way you'll have great views of the Blue Ridge Mountains, see some Texas longhorns, and visit at the site of the former railroad stop that bypassed Middleburg, fueling Middleburg's earlier decline.

The Virginia Gold Cup, held the first Saturday in May, is so important to the local steeplechase circuit that other races are held based on the number of weekends between them and the premier event. For example, steeplechase races at Middleburg's Glenwood Park are held five Saturdays before the Virginia Gold Cup.

Rest assured, this is "the place to be" that May weekend if you are interested in steeplechase racing. Of course, if flat racing is your thing, you'll be at the Kentucky Derby, held the same day. The crowd usually stays around Great Meadow until late afternoon to hear the Derby broadcast over the public address system. The day is one of contrasts: elegant, catered banquets for those on Member's Hill; somewhat less-lavish railside parties sponsored by corporations, where lobbyists hope to speak with congressional bigwigs in a friendly environment; and thousands of everyday horse lovers just

NORTH

MIDDLEBURG

R
Park &
START

50

709

Landmark School Rd.

Zulla Rd.

626

629

686

Meredyth Vineyards

628

Landmark Rd.

679

626

The Plains Rd.

Dr. Lear Rd.

707

Bunker Hill Rd.

55

763

THE PLAINS
R

709

245

55

750

GREAT MEADOW

HOW to get there
Take Route 66 west to Route 50 (exit 57). Follow Route 50 for approximately 20 miles to town of Middleburg. Turn right at only stoplight onto Route 626, Foxcroft Road. Park in elementary school lot.

DIREC-TIONS for the ride

- Left out of school lot to stoplight.
- Right on Route 50 through Middleburg.
- Left on Zulla Road, Route 709.
- Left onto Route 707, unmarked Dr. Lear Road.
- Right onto Route 55.
- Left onto Bunker Hill Road, Route 763
- Left onto Route 55; immediate Left on Route 709.
- Left on Route 750, Fairfax/Harrison Road.
- At T, right 0.75 mile to visit Great Meadow.
- Retrace route on Route 245 back to T.
- Continue on Route 245 to The Plains.
- Right/left on Route 55 in The Plains onto Route 626.
- At Halfway, right on 679, Landmark Road.
- Bear left onto 628 TRO Landmark Road.
- Optional tour of Meredyth Vineyards on left.
- Left TRO Landmark Church at Route 629.
- Left on Landmark School Road, Route 776.
- Cross Route 50 at stoplight.
- Straight onto Foxcroft Road into parking lot.

out for a day of fun with home-packed picnics and general admission tickets.

The Virginia Gold Cup, around since 1925, has been run near Warrenton most of that time. When its Warrenton home was lost to development, a foundation was formed, Great Meadow was acquired, and the Gold Cup moved there in 1984. The land has a permanent, scenic easement, ensuring a place to enjoy such races in the future. Proceeds from the Gold Cup assist local charities and provide operating expenses so that the land may be used year-round by nonprofit organizations.

As you ride on Route 750 just before Great Meadow, be on the lookout for some Texas longhorns. They are rare in these parts—and an interesting deviation from the horse and cattle farms. After visiting the home of the Gold Cup, ride north through The Plains, where you'll be on nearly flat ground. This is where the railroad line came out from Alexandria. A favorite rest stop of local cyclists here is The Rail Stop, where you can get a bite to eat and a close-up look at a stuffed red fox sitting right in the window. Farther north, you'll go through Halfway and past the Meredyth Vineyards, described in Ride 28.

Historic Waterford

Distance:	47 miles
Approximate pedaling time:	4 hours
Terrain:	Rolling and hilly
Surface:	Paved two-lane roads, bike paths
Things to see:	Historic Waterford and Lincoln
Facilities:	Stores in Purcellville, Waterford
Recommended for:	Tourists, Natural beauty, Countryside, Workout

Although this ride starts from Middleburg, energetic riders seeking to link together several rides and make a long weekend out of touring the Virginia Hunt Country could use the Washington and Old Dominion (W & OD) bike path out to Purcellville and pick up this route, linking it with other rides from Middleburg. There are a few reasonably priced bed & breakfast inns near Purcellville, and several more-expensive ones in Middleburg.

The ride takes you through some of Loudoun County's historic towns. The county was formed from Fairfax County and was named for John Campbell, fourth Earl of Loudoun. Although he was named the commander of British forces in North America during an early part of the French and Indian War and was governor of Virginia from 1756 to 1759, he never actually came to the colonies. It was not uncommon for lieutenant governors to be the on-site representatives of nobility, and this was no exception.

On the way, you first pass through Purcellville. This town is west of Leesburg and provided services to travelers on their way to Snickers Gap to reach Winchester or Harpers Ferry. The railroad came in 1874, causing the town to prosper. As you ride along Main Street, you will

WATERFORD
R

Factory St.

9

662

Clark's Gap Rd.

Hamilton Station Rd. 704

Hancher Ave.

W & OD bike path

PAEONIAN SPRINGS

PURCELLVILLE
R

7

Simpson Circle Rd.

Lincoln Rd.

NORTH

690

722

728

North Fork Rd.

734

731

611

Water Mill Rd.

St. Louis Rd.

Snickersville Pike

734

Foxcroft
School Rd.

Sam Fred Rd.

626

748

50

MIDDLEBURG
R

Park &
START

HOW
to get
there

Take Route 66 west to Route 50
(exit 57). Follow Route 50 for
approximately 20 miles to town of
Middleburg. Turn right at only stoplight
onto Route 626, Foxcroft Road. Park in
elementary school lot. Option: Bike out to
Purcellville on the W & OD path.

DIREC-TIONS for the ride

- Right out of school lot onto Foxcroft Road, Route 626.
- Straight at Pot House Road.
- Right on St. Louis Road, Route 611.
- At light, straight onto Route 690.
- At T, right on Business Route 7 into Purcellville.
- Left at Hancher Avenue.
- Right onto W & OD bike path.
- Left on Hamilton Station Road, Route 704.
- Left on Route 662, Clark's Gap Road.
- Left on Factory Street, into Waterford.
- Return on Factory Street to Route 662.
- Right on 662, Clark's Gap Road.
- Right on Route 9 and immediate left onto Simpson Circle Road.
- Right onto W & OD bike path in Paeonian Springs.
- Bear left on Maple Avenue, Route 727, into Purcellville.
- Cross Route 7 onto Lincoln Road, Route 722.
- Right on North Fork Road, Route 728.
- Left on Water Mill Road, Route 731.
- Left on Snickersville Turnpike, Route 734.
- Bear right TRO Snickersville at Route 733.
- Right on Sam Fred Road, Route 748.
- Right on Route 50 (busy, stay right).
- Right at stoplight back to school parking lot.

see many Victorian-style homes resulting from that prosperity.

Arriving in Waterford, note the marker stating that the entire village of Waterford, Virginia, was designated a National Historic Landmark in 1970, one of only three such landmarks in the United States. The village, founded by Quakers from Pennsylvania, was not affected by changing trends or automation, and residents maintained most of their traditional farming methods for many years. As a result, most structures are true to their origins. Limited restoration and preservation is overseen by The Waterford Foundation.

The Civil War brought strange times to Waterford. Reflecting their Quaker upbringing, most residents were opposed to slavery and voted 221 to 36 against secession. Samuel C. Means, owner of the mill, formed the Loudoun Rangers and led hit-and-run warfare against the Confederates similar to John Mosby's raids against Union troops. The Loudoun Rangers were the only organized unit of Virginians to fight on the side of the Union. Yet, this being Virginia, some locals also joined the Confederacy, leading to one of the more unusual stories of the Civil War.

On August 26, 1862, Means's company arrived at Waterford and occupied the Baptist church. That night they were attacked by part of a Virginia battalion composed of men from Loudoun County. The battle raged for three hours, leaving dead and wounded on both sides. Cease fires were called twice, and a local woman entered the church to communicate Confederate demands of surrender. Finally, nearly out of ammunition, Means's company surrendered. Despite the surrender, William Snoots, a Confederate soldier, maintained his right to shoot a particular Loudoun Ranger: Charles Snoots, his brother. It took the intervention of a Confederate officer to stop him. Such was the hatred engendered by that war.

Today Waterford is best known for its annual homes tour and crafts exhibit, Virginia's oldest juried crafts fair, held the first weekend in October. Houses built by Quakers are open for tours, and there is an archeological display and limited excavation of the late-eighteenth century tannery operation. This house tour and arts and crafts festival is extremely popular; traffic and parking are terrible. However, I've used this bike route to lead club rides to the fair. Just use Route 704 out and back, and you'll avoid most traffic.

On the return route along the W & OD bike path, you'll pass through Paeonian Springs, which was once a spa. A lake was fed by mineral springs, and the water was shipped all over the United States. The town was named for Paeon Aesculapius, Greek god of medicine. On this section of the bike path, you might sight wild turkeys in the spring. If you are riding in the fall, keep your eyes open for hairy woodpeckers.

Your next historic town will be Lincoln, another Quaker settlement. The townspeople were historically against slavery, and it is reported that the first meeting of the Manumission and Emigration Society was held here in the Goose Creek schoolhouse as early as 1824. Under the leadership of Yardley Taylor, the community was actively involved with the Underground Railroad.

The return route will follow parts of the Snickersville Turnpike, a winding, narrow road over Hibbs Bridge with stone walls flanking one or both sides. The road is currently designated a Virginia Scenic Byway, and local residents are seeking to increase its preservation status to guard against plans of the Virginia Department of Transportation to widen and straighten it into a commuter route, which would eliminate most of its character and some of the centuries-old walls. There is at least one "hill of note" on this road; I'm sure you'll figure out which one I mean!

Bicycling Organizations in the D.C. Area

Bicycle Federation of America
1506 21st Street N.W.
Suite 200
Washington, D.C. 20036
(202) 463–6622
http://www.bikefed.org

National nonprofit group that promotes safe bicycle use.

League of American Bicyclists
1612 K Street N.W.
Suite 401
Washington, D.C. 20006
(202) 822–1333
http://www.bikeleague.org/

The nation's oldest nonprofit organization representing cyclists in the United States. Sponsors the National Bike Month (May) and founded the International Police Mountain Bike Association.

Potomac Chapter of American Youth Hostels
1108 K Street N.W.
Washington, D.C. 20005
(202) 783–4943
http://www.hiayh.org/council/va.htm

Local chapter of national group runs bike trips of one day or more, operates downtown youth hostel and bike/outdoors shop, plans rides to other hostels in the region.

Potomac Pedalers Touring Club
6729 Curran Street
McLean, VA 22101
(202) 363–8687
http://www.cyberider.us.net/bikes/PPTC.html

With more than 4,500 members, the Potomac Pedalers Club is the largest recreational cycling organization in the Washington area. The group runs weekly rides and tours, published in their monthly newsletter, "Pedal Patter."

Washington Area Bicyclist Association
1511 K Street
Suite 1015
Washington, D.C. 20005
(202) 628–2500
http://www.waba.org/

A group that advocates improved trails and routes for bicycle commuters. Also operates a warehouse for maps and cycling books.

Regional Conservation Groups

Audubon Naturalist Society
8940 Jones Mill Road
Chevy Chase, MD 20815
(301) 652–9188
http://www.audubonnaturalist.org

Local environmental organization that offers many educational programs.

Potomac Appalachian Trail Club
118 Park Street S.E.
Vienna, VA 22180
(703) 242–0315
http://www.patc.simplenet.com/

Local nonprofit group dedicated to creating and preserving hiking trails in the Mid-Atlantic region.

Maps to Obtain

ADC's Washington Area Bike Map. Compiled by Metropolitan Washington Council of Governments. $10.95. Available at bookstores and newsstands.

Arlington, Virginia, Bikeway Map and Guide. Published by the Arlington County Department of Public Works. Free. Contact Public Works Planning Division, No. 1 Court House Plaza, 2100 North Clarendon Boulevard, Arlington, VA 22201. (703) 228–3681.

D.C. Bikeways. Series of eight maps published by the city. $3.00. Write to D.C. Office of Documents, 441 4th Street N.W., Suite 520, Washington, D.C. 20001. (202) 727–5090.

Maryland Bicycle Touring Map. Free. Available from Office of Tourism Development, 45 Calvert Street, Annapolis, MD 21401.

Station Masters: A Comprehensive Guide to Metrorail Station Neighborhoods. Published by Bowring Cartographic. $3.95. Available at bookstores.

Trails in Montgomery County Parks. Contact Maryland National Capital Parks and Planning Commission (MNCPPC), 8787 Georgia Avenue N.W., Silver Spring, MD 20910. (301) 495–2503.

Virginia Atlas and Gazetteer. Published by DeLorme Mapping Company. Includes topographic maps, hike/bike trails, canoeing areas. $12.95. Available at bookstores.

Washington, D.C., and Vicinity Street Map. Published by ADC. $9.95. Available at bookstores.

W & OD R.R. Regional Park Trail Guide. $5.95. Contact Northern Virginia Regional Park Authority, 5400 Ox Road, Fairfax Station, VA 22039. (703) 352–5900. Also available from the W & OD Trail office at (703) 729–0596 and some bike shops.

Suggested Reading

Abramson, Rudy. *Hallowed Ground: Preserving America's Heritage.* Charlottesville, VA: Thomasson–Grant & Lickle, 1996.

Applewhite, E. J. *Washington, Itself: An Informal Guide to the Capital of the United States.* Second edition. Maryland: Madison Books, 1993.

Bergner, Audrey Windsor. *The Visitor's Guide to Middleburg, Virginia, and the Surrounding John Singleton Mosby Heritage Area.* Virginia: The Middleburg Press, 1997.

Choukas-Bradley, Melanie, and Polly Alexander. *City of Trees: The Complete Field Guide to the Trees of Washington, D.C.* Baltimore: The Johns Hopkins Press, 1987.

Colbert, Judy and Ed. *Virginia: Off the Beaten Path.* Fifth edition. Old Saybrook, CT: The Globe Pequot Press, 1998.

Hahn, Thomas F. *Towpath Guide to the C & O Canal.* Freemansburg, PA: American Canal and Transport Society, 1996.

Halle, Louis J. *Spring in Washington.* Baltimore: The Johns Hopkins Press, 1988.

Helfer, Chuck and Gail. *Chuck and Gail's Favorite Rides.* Takoma Park, MD: Cycleways, 1992.

Scheel, Eugene M. *The Hisotry of Middleburg and Vicinity.* Virginia: The Piedmont Press, 1987.

Weeks, Christopher. *AIA Guide to the Architecture of Washington, D.C.* Third edition. Baltimore: The Johns Hopkins Press, 1994.

Wilds, Claudia. *Finding Birds in the National Capital Area.* Washington, D.C.: Smithsonian Institution Press, 1983.

Wurman, Richard Saul. *Washington, D.C. Access: The Capital Guide to the Capital City.* Los Angeles: Access Press, 1989.

Bicycle Rental and Repair Centers in the D.C. Area

Bikes USA, 1506 C Belle View Boulevard, Alexandria, VA (on the Mount Vernon Bike Trail). (703) 768–3444. ATB and hybrids.

Big Wheel Bikes, In Georgetown: 1034 33rd Street N.W., Washington, D.C. (202) 337–0254. On Capitol Hill: 315 Seventh Street S.E., Washington, D.C. (202) 543–1600. In Old Town: 2 Prince Street, Alexandria, VA. (703) 739–2300. In Bethesda: 6917 Arlington Road, Bethesda, MD. (301) 652–0192. All types of bikes.

City Bikes, 2501 Champlain Street N.W., Washington, D.C. (202) 265–1564. Mountain bikes and hybrids.

Fletcher's Boat House, 4940 Canal Road N.W., Washington, D.C. (202) 244–0461. One- and fifteen-speed bikes. Seasonal.

Metropolis Bike & Scooter, Inc. On Capitol Hill: 709 8th Street S.E., Washington, D.C. (202) 543–8900. In Arlington: 4056 South 28th Street (The Village at Shirlington), Arlington, VA. (703) 671–1700. ATB and hybrids.

Potomac Outdoors, 7687 MacArthur Boulevard, Cabin John, MD. (301) 320–1544. ATB and hybrids.

Spinnaker 'n' Spoke, at the Washington Sailing Marina (Daingerfield Island), on the Mount Vernon Bike Path. (703) 548–9027. One- and fifteen-speed bikes. Seasonal.

Swain's Lock, about 2.5 miles west of Great Falls on the C & O Canal. (301) 299–9006. One-speed bikes; tandems. Seasonal.

Thompson Boat Center, Rock Creek Parkway & Virginia Avenue N.W., Washington, D.C. (202) 333–4861. One- and twenty-one-speed bikes, kids' bikes. Seasonal.

Washington Bike Center (Reston Town Center), 11932 Democracy Drive, Reston, VA. (703) 742–7775. Hybrids.

Obtaining a Metrorail Bike-on-Rail Permit

Many of these rides can begin at Metrorail stations, especially helpful for those living in the city without owning a car. However, you cannot simply show up at the nearest Metro station with your bike and board the train to your desired destination. A Bike-on-Rail permit is currently required. Also, bikes are permitted on Metrorail only at certain times and on certain days.

Generally, bicycles are permitted all day on weekends and on weekdays between 10:00 A.M. and 2:00 P.M. and after 7:00 P.M. No bicycles may be allowed on Metrorail on certain busy weekends or holidays. Bikes are permitted only in the last car of each train, and no more than four bikes are allowed per train.

To obtain a permit, you need to visit either the Metro headquarters at 800 Fifth Street N.W., Washington, D.C., or certain urban stations. Call ahead to determine when each is open (202–962–1051). You'll be given a booklet containing all the safety instructions and rules when bikes are allowed, then given a short test on this information. After passing the test and paying a $15 processing fee, you'll be presented with a photo identification card good for three years. The permit only allows you to use the system; you still have to purchase a farecard like other passengers.

Beginning in May 1998, Metro began a six-month test eliminating the need for a Bike-on-Rail permit. Depending on the outcome, you may not need one, or the rules may be changed. Call (202) 962–1051 for the latest information before attempting to use Metrorail with your bike. You may also visit their Web site at http://www.wmata.com.

Organized Bike Rides Around D.C.

If you prefer riding with lots of other cyclists, there are a number of organized rides near Washington you might wish to join; notably, multiday rides in Maryland and Virginia. These are held annually, with a new route each year. Unfortunately, it isn't safe for large numbers of cyclists to compete with traffic on D.C. roads, so there are few commercial rides actually in D.C.

An exception is Bike the Sites, which leads small groups around the Mall and on the Mount Vernon Trail. Bike rentals are included in the price. Information is available at (202) 966–8662 or http://www.bikethesites.com.

Bike Virginia organizes a five-day ride through Virginia countryside each year, usually in June. Luggage is transported and riders may camp or stay in nearby motels. Weekend trips are also held a couple of times a year. Contact (757) 229–0507 or http://www.bikevirginia.org.

Cycle Across Maryland offers a week-long ride in a different part of the state each July. Camping or motels are offered. Fat tire weekends are also arranged. Contact (888) CAM–RIDE or http://www.cyclexmd.org.

Fund-raising cycle tours of one or two days are organized by the D.C. Multiple Sclerosis Society. Contact (202) 296–5353 or http://www.dcw.nmss.org. D.C. Habitat for Humanity (202–610–2355) offers a one-day ride. The Maryland Chapter of the MS Society also offers multiday fund-raising rides (800–FIGHT–MS).

Some of the best deals for organized bicycle weekends are offered through the local cycling clubs. The Potomac Peddlers (see *Bike Organizations*) runs weekend events in the spring to Lewes, DE, and summer weekends in the Shenandoah Valley. Their largest event, the Fall Frolic, is held near Hagerstown, MD. The Baltimore Bicycle Club (410–792–8308) also offers excellent weekend events, including the Spring Fling at Chestertown, MD. You don't have to be a member of these organizations to sign up.

Spokes, a free newspaper distributed in most bike shops, lists bicycling events within several hundred miles of Washington, including commercial rides, club events, fund-raisers, and races. You don't have to race; spectators are welcome.

About the Author

Michael Leccese is a writer and editor for *Landscape Architecture* magazine. His articles on architecture, travel, and the environment have appeared in such publications as the *Washington Post, Historic Preservation,* and the *Miami Herald.* He is also the author of Globe Pequot's *Short Bike Rides in Colorado* and the coauthor of *The Bicyclist's Sourcebook: The Ultimate Directory of Cycling Information* (Woodbine House, 1991). An advocate of bicycle commuting, he has toured much of Europe and the United States on two wheels.